The
CREATIVE
H·O·M·E
ORGANIZER

The CREATIVE H·O·M·E ORGANIZER

Emilie Barnes

HARVEST HOUSE PUBLISHERS
Eugene, Oregon 97402

THE CREATIVE HOME ORGANIZER

Copyright © 1988 by Harvest House Publishers
Eugene, Oregon 97402

Library of Congress Catalog Card Number 83-082317
ISBN 0-89081-391-4

Printed in the United States of America.

DEDICATION

This book is dedicated to the many women in the United States and Canada who have mailed me their helpful hints on organizing their homes. The hints and ideas in this book are suggestions to help solve household problems. I cannot guarantee 100 percent success. However, I know from my own personal experience that they do work. Because of the wide variety of contributions, I cannot verify the originality of these ideas and hints.

The contents of this book will save you many hours in research and years in experiences. It is a valuable time-saving resource.

I appreciate all the women who have made this book possible. Many ways to give you "More Hours In Your Day" are contained in this book. As you read this book, may the hours you save give you more valuable time to spend with our Lord and your family.

Moses prayed, "Let the favor of the Lord our God be upon us; and do confirm for us the work of our hands; yes, confirm the work of our hands" (Psalm 90:17 NASB). *Confirm* means "to give meaning, to make permanent." I trust you can see the significance of these ideas in lightening the load of your everyday routine.

I trust that God helps you to see the value of the routine and the importance of what we might consider boring and meaningless—"the same old thing." Let there be joy in your radiance as you learn to lighten your load around the home, and may you recognize the sense of permanence and significance in the monotonous assignments of life. I trust that these ideas will give you "hope to cope" with life.

—Emilie Barnes

CONTENTS

❧

FOREWORD

Emilie has been a special friend of mine for almost 15 years and whenever I go to Emilie's home for dinner, I learn something new. I've found I can spin dry my lettuce in a washing machine and preserve my candles in the freezer. There is no end to Emilie's household hints.

As she shares her ideas with you in this book, you can be assured that each thing she suggests she has tried herself and found it to be practical and time saving. She really wants you to have MORE HOURS IN *YOUR* DAY.

Emilie's home reflects her own creative charm and I can attest to the fact that Emilie practices what she teaches. As you apply her new ideas to your home you will be so excited that you will want Emilie to come to your town to present her program in person.

—Florence Littauer
Redlands, California

The
CREATIVE
H·O·M·E
ORGANIZER

Organization

A place
for everything and
everything in its place

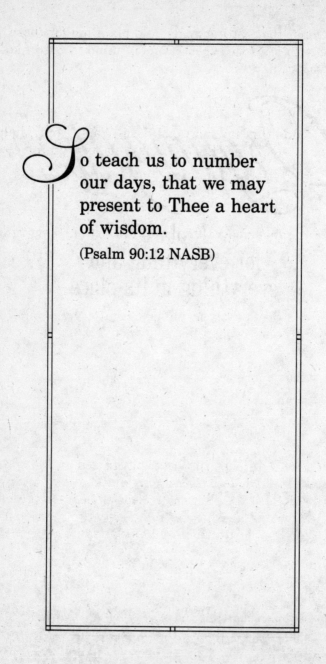

So teach us to number our days, that we may present to Thee a heart of wisdom.

(Psalm 90:12 NASB)

Remember that setting goals, and planning for those goals, with realistic expectations in mind is what makes good things happen.

———————

I have found that my motto, "Do the Worst First," helps me get started. Once the worst is done, everything else is so much easier.

———————

Set short-range goals that build toward your long-range purpose.

———————

Share your goals with people who really care about you and want to help you.

———————

A goal is nothing but a "dream with a deadline."

———————

If you have a difficult time getting started each day, take 15 minutes at the end of each day and make a "to do" list. Write down the items that need to be done the next day. As you start fresh tomorrow you will already have completed the most difficult job of the day—prioritizing your activities.

———————

When people learn that there are few, if any, short cuts to success, many of them cannot cope with the disappointment.

I had so much data and information around the house that I became a slave to recording and keeping track of everything. A friend of mine urged me to look into a small home computer. At first I balked, but I am so glad I heard him out. Now that I have one, I can't believe how valuable the computer has become. A real time saver and organizer.

––––––––

Whenever I receive an invitation to something, I attach the invitation to my kitchen calendar in the month the event will take place. I also write the event on the calendar on the appropriate day. I keep the invitations clipped to the calendar in one stack and in chronological order. After each event has taken place, I remove the invitation. Keeping the invitation handy saves me from searching for the time, the place, and especially the spelling of the names.

––––––––

In your address book, write the names in ink and the addresses in pencil. In this way old addresses can be erased and new ones entered without a mess.

––––––––

In budgeting my time on my daily calendar, I leave a cushion of 15 minutes here and there on my schedule. This way I don't find myself running from one appointment to another.

––––––––

People don't plan to be failures. But they do plan success.

––––––––

I have kept a mini-notebook for several years which I call

"The Lord Provides." In it, I've listed everything that has been given to us as gifts and from whom. Also listed are things we have found and items donated to us. It's beautiful to see how the Lord leads others to meet our needs and desires.

———

If the phone encroaches on your efficiency, unplug it or let it ring. Can't bear that? An answering machine or service will take your messages and let you return calls at your convenience.

———

Keep a pad and pen next to your bed and in your bathroom—jot down ideas, things to do, supplies, and makeup you need.

———

Make a list on paper of ten goals that you wish to attain by the end of the year and do them.

———

Buy a handbag large enough to hold a paperback book or magazine (for waiting time) and a small notebook for list making. Attach your keys to a chain that clips to, or loops around, the strap. Tuck keys inside. Keep cosmetics in a separate bag that closes to keep makeup from falling out. Wrap a rubber band around pens and pencils. Always put your eyeglasses in the same compartment. Remove notes, crumpled tissues, deposit slips, and the like once a week or so, maybe while you watch TV. Switch bags only when you dress up.

———

Take time to play or do a fun activity. Sometimes you

have to schedule time for yourself. This is important to your success in all your other activities.

Don't keep an address book for home use. Instead, buy a small 3 x 5 file box. Use 3 x 5 cards to list names alphabetically and file them in the box. You'll never lose the box or spend money replacing old address books. When someone moves or changes a phone number, just replace the card. Add cards when needed.

When paperwork begins to mount, start a tickler file. Purchase a cardboard file box. Make a file for each day of the month. Then organize your file. As papers, appointments, and deadlines come in, file them in their appropriate file. Events several months ahead are filed by month initially. At the beginning of that month, papers are filed under the appropriate day, using the daily files from last month's folders. Each morning, pull out the day's file and organize your day.

When reorganizing your closet, keep all colors together. Example: Blouses—light to dark; pants—light to dark; shirts; jackets; and so on.

The most basic part of organization is knowing what to throw away. Invite an objective friend over to help make those decisions. Less is better than more. It saves you a lot of cleaning.

It takes time for change to be assimilated.

One working woman wrote, "It's important to look professional and not weighted down when making customer calls. I have one leather briefcase that holds my wallet, makeup, calendar and other business-related files. If I go to lunch and I don't want to take my briefcase, I simply take my wallet and go. No more fumbling with briefcase, purse, keys, etc."

————

Save space by putting long-handled kitchen utensils in a ceramic crock by the stove. This will save drawer space.

————

Once you've organized your space, you have to keep it organized by maintaining the space on a regular basis. I find the maintenance part of organization is the most important aspect.

————

When storing keepsakes or clothing, number your boxes 1, 2, 3, and so on. Make out a 3 x 5 card and list on it what you're storing in the numbered boxes. File your 3 x 5 cards in a file box. When you need to look for an item, simply go to your file box and find the card with the item listed. Check the card number and get your box down. Item found in minutes.

————

Use a kitchen cutlery tray to store art supplies, children's crayons, pencils, etc.

————

Use colored plastic rings to color code your keys. It makes it much easier to locate keys.

If you travel often, always keep a duplicate makeup and toiletry bag packed. Then you'll have soap, shampoo, lotion, toothbrush, makeup, comb, and brush ready to go. It saves time and serves as a backup in case you run out of something.

The busy person's greatest need is for "effective," not "efficient," planning. Being effective means choosing the right task from all the alternatives. Being efficient means doing any job that happens to be around. The importance of planning is, it saves you time in the end. Know what you have to do and have your priorities established.

Get rid of extra paper. Almost 90 percent of the paper in your home or office is never referred to again. Get rid of as much of it as possible.

Have a secret shelf for gifts. When you find something on sale or have time to shop, buy gifts in quantity and wrap and tag them for future giving.

Many household chores can be done during "in-between times"—in between outings, appointments, or TV programs. Once you realize that it takes only 15 minutes to change the sheets, you can fit this and similar tasks into the available time slots.

Color code your files for a real time-saver. The red folders can be for "hot" items, and so forth. The bright colors will cheer up any area.

———————

I find that if I break a project into a lot of small jobs and complete the little pieces, I get the job done faster. At times I even reward myself with a treat for doing a good job.

———————

We realize that we are responsible for causing our own effects in life. We tackle the toughest, most challenging assignment in our lives, first understanding that our gratification will come after we have made the effort to do the job.

———————

Take time to decide to make the time to do what you want and need to make your life what you want it to be.

———————

Studies show that the success rate for people who write down their goals is about 90 times greater than for those who don't.

———————

You must be positive in your approach to organization. Make a list; eliminate what you don't need. Set a schedule; eliminate interruptions. Be positive about being organized. Remember you are in charge. Total organization doesn't exist. Organization is a lifetime process. You are capable of handling your flow of appointments, clothes, money, and so forth.

If you cannot find time to do what you want, here is how to make time: 1. Delegate some of the household work to other family members. 2. Eliminate some of the work entirely. (You don't have to iron certain items that you do.) 3. Make sure all your children contribute to running the household. 4. Use small amounts of time (five to ten minutes) to your best advantage. 5. Carefully plan the use of leisure time. Concentrate on doing those activities that give you real pleasure. 6. Leave yourself some open-ended time for a spur-of-the-moment activity. Do not cram your appointment book full of things to do.

Do you seem to have a lot of spare time or have trouble making good use of your spare time? You might consider learning a new skill or cultivating a new friendship. Check your local newspaper to find some groups you could attend that would interest you, or become a volunteer in some capacity.

Simplify your life. Get rid of the clutter and the nonproductive activities.

To keep track of your credit cards, lay them out and photocopy them. All the info is on one sheet.

It is not what you get that makes you successful; it is what you are continuing to do with what you've got.

It's not what you are that holds you back; it's what you think you are not.

When I have to decide if I'm going to discard something (or give it away), I ask myself, "Do I need the item or want the item?" If I answer "want," that usually tells me I might very well get rid of the item.

Remember that your goal is to get organized so that you can work toward your mission in life.

I practice a 45/15 rule that really helps me. It works like this. After every 45-minute work cycle I take a 15-minute break and do something different—take a short walk, go outside for some fresh air, call someone on the phone, get a drink of water. This rule keeps me renewed and fresh.

You get out what you put in. There's no such thing as a free lunch.

When you are away on vacation or are away from your home for a period of time: 1. Instruct the post office to hold your mail until you return. 2. Stop deliveries of papers, milk, and so forth. 3. Buy a timer and hook it up so that a light goes on at dusk and off at midnight. 4. Inform a trusted neighbor that you will be away and have him look after your home. 5. Invite a friend or college student to stay at your house while you are away.

Having more than one phone can be a frustration as well as a convenience, so I keep a list of frequently called numbers beside each of my phones. Emergency numbers and those of close relatives are a must if you live alone, even if you normally remember the numbers. In a stressful situation, you might forget.

———

Make a list of three things you want to do. Next to each item write two reasons why you are not doing it. Change the two negatives into two positives. The ability to turn a negative attitude into a positive one is the key to self-organization.

———

An easy way to organize your handbag is to have separate little purses—one for cosmetics, one for food items (like mints, gum, suckers, dental floss), one for bits of papers and business cards. Another can be for Band-Aids, nail clippers, nail file, nail polish, pills. You can go on and on. All these little bags go into your large handbag. Then when you want to change purses, just take out whichever bags you need and you are ready to go.

———

Never have time to read all the magazine articles that you would like? When you receive a magazine, quickly go through and tear out the articles you find interesting and file away for later reading.

———

Five minute pickup. Pick up and dust in each room for five minutes. Time yourself with a kitchen timer.

❧

Plan more—think more—work more.

Money & Time Saving Ideas

The homemaker's helpers

*S*he is energetic, a hard
worker, and watches
for bargains. She works
far into the night!

(Proverbs 31:17,18)

Banks are now offering customers a wide range of account alternatives, such as super savings and money market accounts and certificates of deposit. Choose the right account to suit your needs by asking yourself: Can I write checks against the account? Are service charges involved? How much interest is earned? Are earnings determined at a fixed rate or does the rate vary? If I withdraw funds, is there a penalty? Is there a minimum deposit? Minimum balance? Can accounts be opened or closed over the phone or by using automatic teller machines?

Your money earns interest at different rates, depending on the savings account vehicle that you choose. Regular passbook accounts usually earn less interest than certificates of deposit or money market accounts, for example. Certificates of deposit and money market accounts require you to leave the money on deposit for a specified amount of time. Money put into such accounts usually cannot be withdrawn without penalty.

Some guidelines to help cut your energy bills down to size: 1. Reduce overall lighting in nonworking areas by removing one bulb out of three in multiple light fixtures. 2. Use one large bulb instead of several small ones if bright light is needed. 3. Install dimmer or hi-lo switches when replacing switches. 4. If using a three-way lamp, only use the highest setting when reading. 5. Use white or light-colored lampshades to get maximum light. 6. Prevent water from cooling as it travels to your plumbing fixtures by wrapping hot water pipes with insulating material. 7. Always bring liquids to a boil in a covered pan. 8. Cook with a timer. 9. Use pans made of glass or ceramic rather than metal to reduce cooking temperature.

Here's an easy way to make great fire starters: Save half-gallon cardboard milk cartons, rinse them well, and leave them open to dry. Then stuff them with newspaper and let some of the paper protrude for easy lighting. The paper will set the carton ablaze because of the wax coating, and the carton will burn long enough to ignite the logs.

———

Save margarine and butter wrappers in the freezer, and use them to grease pans and cookie sheets.

———

Last-minute gifts with class: Wrap homemade bread in a festive dish towel, tie with yarn, and include the bread recipe. Keep a bestselling hardcover book on hand and quickly add an inscription on the inside cover. Create your own spice blends. Put the spice mixture in a pretty jar. A green-thumbed friend will appreciate a box of herb seeds and gardening essentials such as peat pots.

———

Many studies show that if you can change a habit or begin a new habit and stick to it for 21 days, you have made a new habit in your life.

———

Know that each moment of your life, once gone, is lost forever.

———

Everyone at one time or another has to buy a gift for that certain someone who has "everything." A "goodie box" can be filled with necessities like medical supplies or toiletries of the person's liking.

————

Save 500 dollars to 1000 dollars a year by not smoking.

————

Save 400 dollars a year by shopping smart. Buy in bulk when items are on sale, not one six-pack at a time at a convenience store.

————

Good food often costs less than junk food and saves on medical bills, vitamin pills, and diet pills.

————

One big time waster in our society is TV. You certainly want to evaluate how you let this appliance deprive you of valuable time slots. You may even consider getting rid of your "time bandit."

————

I found that during the gasoline shortage I had to group my errands in order to save on gasoline. It worked so well then, that I continue to group my errands. I find this saves me a lot of time and money each day.

————

There's no time like the present.

————

The waxed paper used in cereal boxes is great for

greasing pans when baking. You get about four sizeable sheets when cut, and it doesn't tear as easily as purchased waxed paper.

Does a "50 percent off" sign make your heart beat faster? Does your credit card burn a hole in your wallet? Think about upcoming birthdays, anniversaries, and other gift-giving occasions. Buy ahead and have the fun of shopping without wasting money.

Serve food from the pot it's cooked in rather than transferring it to serving bowls. It saves so much time.

Roll piecrust between two sheets of waxed paper. The rolling pin stays clean and there's no flour to contend with.

Cook extra servings whenever possible and freeze in individual portions.

Try to limit your telephone conversations to a minimum of time if they are social calls. Learn to do more than one thing at one time.

As a traveling salesperson, I keep evening meetings to a minimum; however, I do take advantage of breakfast and lunch hours and make appointments during these blocks of time.

———

A sturdy plastic cutting board is not only more sanitary than a wooden board (which absorbs bacteria) but can go right into the dishwasher.

———

One of the best ways I have found to reduce stress is by saying "NO!" A hard word to say at times, but so valuable. Try it.

———

As you read the newspaper, always have a red pen or marker to spot things. I hate to cut out an article or coupon before others have read the paper. Saves time— you can see what you have checked at a glance.

———

When you empty cans, bottles, and containers as you prepare a meal, don't set them on the work surface again. Drop them immediately into the trash can for recycling.

———

Bag conservation. If you want to make a paper, plastic, or fabric shopping bag last longer, place a shoe box lid inside. The lid will help reinforce the bottom.

———

When marketing, shop quickly with a plan of action and organization (using a marketing list). A study showed that after the first half hour in the market women will spend at least 75 cents a minute. So get in and get out.

———————

Since your time is limited, choose to do things that you enjoy or find useful. Don't overload yourself with tasks or responsibilities. Always strive to simplify your life.

———————

Ever since our whole family has been involved in helping out with the housework, the burden has been lifted from my shoulders. Now our family has more time to spend doing things we like to do.

———————

If you are a supervisor or boss, learn to delegate. Moms, as homemakers, don't do anything that someone else in the family can do.

———————

Get up earlier than usual, and give yourself plenty of time to get properly prepared for the day ahead.

———————

To make full use of the catsup in a nearly empty bottle, rinse the bottle out with a little warm water and add the water to baked beans or any dish requiring a tomato base.

———————

Pack a sack lunch if you work away from home. You can save a lot of money over a period of several months.

Buy top-quality vegetables, fruits, and olives to serve in individual dishes. Buy lesser-quality products for soups, casseroles, or salads.

In order to avoid waiting long periods of time in the doctor's office, I take the first appointment in the morning.

Check the labels on whatever you are buying and make sure that it doesn't take special care. Special-care items take up a lot of your time and thus cost you more money.

If the church office is staffed with volunteers (or even if it isn't), the 3 x 5-card-file idea works great. Sectioning office jobs according to DAILY, WEEKLY, MONTHLY, and YEARLY tasks insures that all jobs are covered and eliminates the need for a "supervisor." When the jobs are completed, they should be dated and initialed for reference.

Don't let work pile up. Decide which projects need to be completed and complete them.

Compare prices of different forms of the same food (frozen, fresh, premixed). You may find one form cheaper than another.

If you have to do errands after food shopping, take along

a large Styrofoam picnic container and put cold or frozen items in it to keep them cold. Then you won't worry about the food spoiling.

———

I've found that if I don't make a decision, I waste time handling problems again and again and again. Save time in the future by making the decision today.

———

Make up your grocery list at the same time that you plan a menu, whether it's for two meals or a week of meals.

———

When you find yourself in the store and in doubt about whether you need a certain item for dinner, go ahead and buy it. It is better to have an extra lemon or box of rice than to have to change the menu or go back to the store again.

———

Giving adult and children's clothes to consignment shops is a way to make some small earnings which can be used where most needed in your house.

———

Use a cutlery tray in bathroom drawers to hold hair-brushes, combs, deodorant, toothpaste, and razors. It keeps the drawers neat and orderly.

———

Do the jobs you dislike first. Once you've got those

unpleasant tasks out of your way, you'll find that the rest of your work will be somewhat easier.

———

I receive so many catalogs through the mail that I now shop by phone. It's amazing how much time and money I save. Each catalog seems to specialize in certain styles or fashions.

———

Use coupons for saving on food costs. Newspapers and magazines are loaded with rebates to consumers buying advertised products. File discount cards in a 3 x 5 file box, and after you have made your marketing list go through and pull the appropriate coupons for your shopping trip.

———

Add interest by wrapping gifts in newspaper. A comic section is great for a child's gift. Fashion ads can be used to wrap garments. Theater ads wrap nicely around theater tickets. Use your imagination.

———

Use discontinued wallpaper for wrapping paper. Last year I wrapped the whole family's Christmas gifts for one dollar.

———

I get more things done in a day by hiring others to do errands, baby-sitting, secretarial work, housekeeping, bookkeeping, gardening, and anything else I can afford.

———

As a teacher, I enjoy labeling boxes to organize my school

stuff. I have labeled ten: one box for each month from September through June. Each month I take down the box containing art projects, papers, and holiday projects appropriate to that month. When I clean and take the things down, I just pop them in the right box. Things rarely get misplaced.

———————

Avoid impulse buying. Watch the ads for off-season sales, which can result in significant savings.

———————

With a two-story house and three children I have found it helpful to have a container at the bottom and top of the stairs. It saves time by eliminating unnecessary trips.

———————

Check the phone book for small-appliance repair centers. They will sell you replacement parts or fix your broken appliance at a far lesser cost than that of a new appliance.

———————

When searching the classified ads for employment, or looking for something to purchase, use a colored accent marker to circle the ads you are interested in. This way you will have a quick reference when checking back.

———————

Make a list of birthdays and anniversaries that require the purchase of greeting cards. Take your list to the card shop and purchase all your greeting cards at one time. Add a few sympathy and get-well cards too. Saves time and gasoline.

Set your breakfast table the night before. Children love to do this.

————

Start your meetings on time, even if you have several late arrivals. Other people appreciate your consideration of their efforts in getting to a meeting on time. Don't reward the late arrivers by delaying the start of the meeting.

————

Keep your Christmas cards in a basket next to devotional reading material. Each day when it comes time to pray, take one or two of these cards and pray for the person who sent the card.

————

When I'm preparing to move, I take down wall hangings (pictures, what-have-you's), remove the nails or hooks from the walls at the same time, and tape them to the back of each object. When they go up again, there is no need to look for hangers. They are right with the picture.

————

Keep a calendar or appointment book in your handbag. It will help you to be on time and to remember when and where you have to be.

————

To control the clock better, get up a half hour earlier and decide what you are going to do with the day that is profitable to you and those close to you.

————

Go to the country and buy fresh foods in season from the grower. They will taste better and cost less.

Cook a large amount of regular rice. Freeze it in family portions. To serve, just put it in a sieve and run hot water through it. It's ready in a jiffy. This is much cheaper than instant rice.

―――――――

Teach yourself to make up one side of the bed at a time. It takes practice but saves precious time and steps.

―――――――

Ever have a problem with your family arriving late for meals? Ring a bell or blow a whistle to give a two-minute warning. They can finish whatever they are doing and arrive on time.

―――――――

A woman from Arizona suggested that when handling rebates, special offers, and mail orders that sometimes never come (and your money is not returned), keep a ledger or file with date and address to whom sent, amount of money sent, and expected date for return of item or rebate (i.e., four to six weeks). Then when it does come, check it off your ledger. Also, note on your cancelled check when the company cashed it. If return postage is guaranteed, make sure you get it back from the company.

―――――――

When entering the kitchen to prepare a meal, fill the sink with hot, sudsy water. All used dishes can soak until time to wash or load the dishwasher.

―――――――

Carry gummed address labels in your purse. Good for

putting on photo envelopes or bank deposit slips and giving to people who want your address. Saves a lot of time.

To prevent the last few postage stamps on a roll from getting stuck together or lost, I place them on envelopes I can use for letter writing or paying bills.

An emergency repair for the missing screw in your glasses is to insert a wooden toothpick through the hinge. Break off both ends of the toothpick and you are in business for a while.

I use my appliances to help beat high heating costs during winter months. After cooking food in the oven, I leave the door open. This puts out quite a bit of heat. I do the same for the clothes dryer. I also open the dishwasher and pull out the racks of steaming hot dishes.

Don't shop for food if you are hungry. You will buy more.

Shop carefully. Compare weights and contents of packages. Take a small hand calculator with you to the market so you can determine the cost per ounce or pound.

Use stewed chicken or turkey (picked off the bones) in casseroles, salads, sandwiches, and creamed dishes.

Roast a large turkey and slice it in family-size portions to freeze for quick lunches and dinners. Turkey is usually the cheapest meat per pound available. Buy seasonal specials. Freeze and use later.

———————

Did you know that most supermarkets stock higher-priced items at eye level? The lower-priced items like salt, sugar, flour are below eye level. Also, beware of foods displayed at the end of aisles, as they may look like they are on sale but many times are not.

———————

Read labels and check expiration dates. Buy foods that will be usable for the longest time. Check labels for nutritional information.

———————

Incorporate leftovers into tasty casserole dishes and stews. Do not discard them.

———————

Do your grocery shopping once a week. You will buy less than when you make frequent trips to the store to buy a few things at a time. It is too easy to pick up extras.

———————

Thrift stores are good places to buy inexpensive household items. You'll find a wealth of new and near-new items, like dishes, glasses, shakers, and linens.

———————

Cut down on use of soft drinks, snack food, ready-mixes,

and paper products. These items increase the cost of your food shopping.

———————

If you shop from a grocery list, don't take anyone with you when you shop. The other person will talk you into purchasing "impulse" items that aren't on your master list.

———————

Save TV dinner containers and make your own TV dinners in quantity. Freeze to use when you are in a hurry. Meat loaf, sweet potatoes, mashed potatoes, corn, and green beans are especially good for this.

———————

Buy nonfat dry milk to use in your cooking, especially white sauces. Prepare a quart and keep it in the refrigerator. Mix half with whole milk as an economy.

❧

The problem the average housewife faces is that she has too much month left over at the end of the money.

Food

Tricks
for the table

She gets up before dawn to prepare breakfast for her household, and plans the day's work for her servant girls.

(Proverbs 31:15)

Wrap foods in moisture-proof packaging such as heavy foil, plastic freezer wrap, or freezer bags.

———

To prevent freezer burn, remove as much air as possible before sealing. Never freeze meat in store packaging, since it's neither airtight nor moisture-proof.

———

Store food in a single layer to allow proper air circulation and speed the freezing process; set thermostat at 0° F.

———

Defrost the freezer when frost buildup reaches a thickness of one-quarter inch.

———

To help keep crackers crisp, store them in a cannister with a dry paper towel inside the cover. To recrisp crackers, place them on a cookie sheet in a 250° oven for about ten minutes.

———

Before freezing fresh bagels, cut them in half. When you're ready to use them, they will defrost faster and can even be toasted while they are still frozen.

———

Use a yellow highlighter pen on your favorite recipes.

———

When you have leftover cooked turkey, chicken, or beef,

but not enough for an entire meal, try chopping it into chunks and adding it to soup for a hearty main dish.

The few extra tablespoons of fruit juice left in the bottom of the bottle are a perfect baste for poultry.

Cooking a lot of tacos? Use your dish drainer. It can hold the shells safely upright while you fill them "production line" fast.

Cook asparagus in an old upright coffee percolator.

When placing things in the freezer, be sure to wrap and date. Place new items in the back of the freezer and move older items to the front.

An inexpensive way to make breakfast cereal is to buy an inexpensive brand of corn or wheat flakes and a box of raisins. Each time you have a bowl of cereal, add two scoops of raisins. It really lasts a long time and is much cheaper than the cereal that contains raisins.

An easy way to get catsup to come out of the opening of a full bottle is to turn the bottle upside down and tap the side of the bottle above the neck. This lets air go through the neck of the bottle.

Prolonged exposure to light produces a greenish tinge on potatoes. To prevent this discoloration, store potatoes properly in a dark, humid, well-ventilated place at a cool 45° to 50° F. They should keep for weeks.

————

To easily remove shish kebab meats and vegetables from the skewers, give the skewers a light coating of salad oil or vegetable cooking spray before you put the meat on them. It makes for easy cleanup also.

————

If you want to ripen green tomatoes, put them in a dark cabinet until they turn red. They turn red in just a few days.

————

When you are packaging hamburger, take it off the plastic meat tray and flatten the meat out. Then put it in a freezer bag. You can place flat packages of meat side by side in the freezer, which uses less space.

————

To cut up canned tomatoes quickly, use kitchen shears and snip the tomatoes right in the can.

————

To separate frozen fruits and vegetables easily, put them in a colander and rinse them under hot tap water.

————

Grease and flour baking pans in one step. Thoroughly

mix one-half cup shortening and one-fourth cup all purpose flour or wheat flour; then use a pastry brush to apply the coating to the pans. Store any leftovers in a covered jar at room temperature.

———————

You can make your own convenience foods. Chop large batches of onion, green pepper, or nuts and freeze them in small units. Grate a week's or month's worth of cheese, then freeze it in recipe-size portions. Shape ground meat or ground turkey into patties so you can thaw a few at a time. Freeze homemade casseroles, soups, stews, and chilies in serving-size portions for faster thawing and reheating.

———————

No need to boil those lasagna noodles anymore! Just spread sauce in the bottom of the pan, place hard, uncooked noodles on top and spread sauce on top of noodles. Continue with the other layers, finishing with noodles and sauce. Cover with foil and bake at 350° for 1 hour 15 minutes.

———————

To lock in freshness and keep those potato chip and corn chip bags closed, simply roll down the top and secure with a clothespin or large paper clip.

———————

To avoid the messy overuse of corn oil in frying, obtain a small plastic hair-coloring container and snip the top off, fill with oil, and squirt a bit wherever needed in your skillet.

———————

Heads of garlic kept too long will dry out or rot, but not if you treat them right. Skin each of the cloves and store them in the refrigerator in a jar of corn or olive oil. Take out cloves as needed and use some of the garlic-flavored oil in cooking or in salad dressing.

———————

Mushrooms slice easily and quickly when you use an egg slicer.

———————

Semi-hard and hard cheeses (such as cheddar) will slice poorly and will crumble once frozen.

———————

Two cubes of sugar stored with any cheese in an airtight container will help to retard the growth of mold.

———————

All cheeses are more flavorful at room temperature than when cold; however, hard cheeses are easier to slice while still cold.

———————

Frozen foods have a definite freezer life; it is important to use the food within the specified period of time. The easiest way to mark meat and other frozen foods is to put a "use by" date on a label or on the package. Your market does this and it makes good sense.

———————

For quick, easy cleanup when preparing sticky hot cereal or steaming rice, coat the inside of the saucepan with vegetable cooking spray beforehand.

Cooking with hot peppers? Handle with care! Hot peppers, also known as chilies and frequently used in Mexican dishes, contain a colorless substance called capsaicin that can seriously irritate skin and eyes. Wear rubber gloves and avoid touching your face or eyes. Wash the gloves and your hands thoroughly afterward.

Make sure your refrigerator and freezer are at the proper temperature; 40° or less for the refrigerator and 0° or less for the freezer.

After opening, refrigerate wheat germ, pure maple syrup, vegetable shortening, salad dressing, jams, jellies, and shelled nuts.

In warm weather (unless your kitchen is air-conditioned) consider storing whole-grain flours, crackers, and breads in the refrigerator or freezer, unless you can use them quickly.

Sometimes (usually on weekends) we order out for pizza, chicken, hamburgers, deli-platters. They even deliver. It really saves us valuable time when preparing food. Be sure to watch your paper for discount coupons.

For many years I have made a favorite sandwich spread that goes over great. Simply mix six ounces of softened cream cheese with one-half cup of mayonnaise. Stir in one-half cup chopped pecans, one cup sliced salad olives, two tablespoons liquid from the olive jar, and a dash of pepper, but NO salt. Mix well.

Make up your own TV dinners. Use containers purchased in your market for microwave or regular ovens. Then put your leftovers in sections of the trays and freeze. Great for Dad and children when Mom's away.

To quickly remove water from the lettuce greens that you have just washed, simply put into a clean pillowcase or lingerie bag and spin in your washing machine for two minutes. Remove from the bag and tear lettuce making a big salad. Store in refrigerator for up to two weeks.

Honey keeps best in a warm, dark place.

After making pies or buns (pastry), I sprinkle the counter with salt. The counter wipes off easily and the dough does not stick to your dishcloth.

Keep parsley fresh and crisp. Wash the parsley and put a bunch of sprigs into a jar, stem ends down. Pour in an inch or two of cold water, enough for the stems to stand in without the leaves touching the water. Tighten the lid, set the jar in the refrigerator, and enjoy crisp parsley for up to two weeks.

Many of our friends and family members have broken the

mealtime salt habit. When I have guests for dinner and set out salt and pepper shakers, I also place a small dish of lemon and lime wedges on the table as a healthy seasoning alternative.

———

Brown sugar won't harden if you store it in the freezer.

———

To make your own pancake syrup, boil equal parts of water, brown sugar, and white sugar. Add two tablespoons butter and presto, buttery syrup.

———

Make up master grocery lists. Many "MORE HOURS IN MY DAY" seminar women make theirs according to the floor plan of their personal market so that the list is in proper order for the place they shop.

———

When freezing foods and liquids in jars, be sure to leave 1½ inches of air at the top to allow for expansion.

———

When you have leftover pastry from making pie crust, roll it into a ball, put it in a plastic bag and freeze. Later, you can make a cobbler very easily by grating this frozen pastry over seasoned, sugared fruit, such as apples or peaches, and baking it.

———

A piece of lettuce dropped into a pot of soup will soak up

the excess grease. Remove the lettuce as soon as it has absorbed the grease.

If your hollandaise sauce starts to curdle, just drop in an ice cube and continue stirring. The sauce will be smooth and creamy again.

When your baked potato is done and dinner isn't quite ready, simply wrap each potato in foil, shiny side inside, and it will keep hot another 45 minutes.

To speed up baking potatoes, simply put a clean nail through the potato. It will cook in half the time.

When using my grater, I put masking tape or a bandage on my thumb.

When you need baked potatoes in a hurry, boil potatoes until nearly done. Then wrap in foil and finish in oven.

To make muffins or cupcakes all the same size, use an ice cream scoop to measure out the batter.

Put leftover rice in a greased casserole and cover with cheese sauce. Sprinkle with grated cheese and bake at

350° for 20 minutes. Use leftover rice in stuffing as a substitute for bread.

Leftover pancakes or waffles? Don't discard them—pop them into the toaster or oven for a quick and easy breakfast or after-school snack.

Our family loves BLT (bacon, lettuce, and tomato) sandwiches. Whenever I fry or microwave bacon, I cook a few extra pieces and put them into a plastic freezer bag and freeze. They are ready for the next BLT sandwich.

Run stale bread through a blender to make bread crumbs. Store in the freezer.

To avoid contamination of food in containers, always use a clean utensil to scoop out mayonnaise, peanut butter, tomato paste, and the like.

To reduce contact with air, store foods and leftovers in the smallest possible containers. This will also make more room in the fridge.

While brewing a fresh pot of coffee, fill two thermos bottles with hot tap water to heat the insides. You will always have a "fresh" hot cup of coffee without having to use extra electricity, and you will reduce the risk of "off" tasting coffee.

––––––––––

The heels of a loaf of bread are not choice pieces in our family, so I set them aside in a paper bag to dry, or toast them. These are used later in meat loaf or casseroles.

––––––––––

Store the remainder of a banana (unpeeled) in a tightly closed jar in the refrigerator. Believe it or not, it won't turn dark.

––––––––––

To disinfect wooden chopping surfaces, scrub with a mild bleach solution, rinse and rub with a thin coat of mineral or salad oil.

––––––––––

An easy way to make bread crumbs is to take frozen hamburger buns and scrape the inside of the bun with a dinner fork.

––––––––––

When canning jams, use Saran Wrap stretched tightly over the mouth of the jar. Then screw the lid on tightly. No need to use paraffin again. One woman has used this method successfully for over ten years.

––––––––––

I put frozen melon balls in punch instead of taste-diluting ice cubes. The melon balls add color and flavor to the drinks, and getting a piece of fruit in your glass is nicer than getting ice.

When I have a few crumbs left in a bag of potato chips or box of crackers, I save them. After I lightly coat them with butter and toast them in the oven until brown, they make a tasty topping for casseroles and baked vegetables.

To help keep a vegetable salad from becoming soggy, place a saucer upside down in the bottom of the bowl before filling it with the ingredients.

If you make dip that's too runny, add some bread crumbs for extra body and flavor.

Bring limp celery back to life by immersing in ice-cold water for just a few hours.

For the two of us I bake six large potatoes. We eat them baked the first night. The second serving is sliced and fried in a bit of butter. The last two potatoes are cubed and served in a cream sauce with some cheese.

You can make your own condensed milk. To $\frac{1}{2}$ cup of boiling water, add 3 tablespoons of butter or margarine, $\frac{1}{2}$ cup of sugar, $1\frac{1}{2}$ cups of powdered milk. Beat all together. Makes $1\frac{1}{3}$ cups.

I have found this hint very helpful when preparing graham crackers or wafers for a crumb crust. I place the crackers in a plastic bag and use the side of my meat tenderizer hammer to pound the crackers into crumbs. All the mess stays confined inside the bag, and I can pour the crumbs into my baking pan.

———

When a recipe calls for dry ingredients, cooking oil, and honey or syrup, always measure the dry ingredients first, then the oil followed by the honey. In this way, your measuring cup stays clean for the next ingredient. The dry ingredients won't stick to the cup and, as the honey is measured last, it will flow freely since the cup was first coated with oil.

———

To avoid a pot boil-over, apply a thin coat of cooking oil around the top of the inside of your pot.

———

A great way to clean fresh mushrooms is to add three to four tablespoons of flour to a medium-size bowl of cold water. Wash the mushrooms in the water. The dirt adheres to the flour particles almost like magic. The mushrooms come out very clean.

———

Put a drop of vegetable or salad oil in boiling water before adding macaroni, noodles, or spaghetti. The oil keeps them from sticking together.

———

Don't throw away a soup or stew that has turned out too

salty. Instead, add a cut raw potato, and discard the potato slices when they are cooked. The potato will absorb most of the salt.

_____

For perfectly shaped fried eggs, press a drinking glass into the center of a slice of bread, and cut out a circle. Place the bread flat in a buttered frying pan. Break an egg into the center of the hole.

_____

Freeze day-old bakery items such as breads, rolls, pastries, cakes. It keeps them fresh and they thaw quickly.

_____

Quickly refrigerate cooked foods and leftovers—reheat thoroughly.

_____

Prepare potluck, picnic-type foods far enough ahead so they can be thoroughly cooled in the refrigerator before being transported.

_____

If you've overestimated the hotcake or waffle appetite of your family, you needn't discard the leftover batter. Cook it up, but brown it very lightly. Freeze with foil between, then pop in the toaster or oven on a morning when you don't have time to cook.

_____

Prepare celery and carrot sticks ahead of time when you

are not hungry. Place them in a jar of water in the refrigerator. They will be crisp when you want them.

———

Have some cooked meat left over, but not enough for an entire meal? Chop it up small, add a small amount of mayonnaise, bell pepper, celery, etc., and you have a great salad for sandwiches.

———

Don't forget to use your microwave, even when making a conventional recipe. Let it melt butter and chocolate, soften cheese, toast nuts, cook bacon, and thaw frozen vegetables.

———

Make your own cracker crumbs in your blender.

———

Make oat flour by whirling oatmeal in a blender. Use for crumb crust in pie. To make the crust, use 1 cup oat flour, 1/4 cup butter or margarine, 2 teaspoons sugar. Blend together with fork.

———

To get more juice out of a lemon, place it in a microwave oven for 30 seconds. Squeeze the lemon and you will get twice as much juice. Vitamins won't be destroyed.

———

This has been a helpful hint for New Englanders: Before dropping a live lobster in a pot of boiling water, gently rub its head in a circular motion between and above the eyes. This relaxes its body and it will go limp. It is now ready to be dropped in the water without a splash or a kick, as it will remain calm. This prevents the usual kicking and boiling water splashes. It also seems easier for the lobster.

———————

Freeze lunch box sandwiches. They can be made up by the week. Put on all ingredients except lettuce. It will save time and trouble.

———————

Read your recipes carefully before you begin; then gather the ingredients and utensils you will need.

———————

Be sure to keep a good supply of staple foods for last-minute meals.

———————

Chill foods quickly by placing them in the freezer for 20 to 30 minutes.

———————

You can have delicious pickled eggs very easily: Hard-boil five or six eggs, then place them in cold water to cool off and make peeling easier. After peeling, put the whole eggs in a pickle jar with the leftover pickle juice, close the cap tightly, give the jar a little shake, and refrigerate. Let the eggs stand 8 to 12 hours. The same pickle juice can be used several times over. The eggs are delicious when using kosher pickle juice.

Lemons and limes get hard and dry when left at room temperature or loose in the crisper, but if you refrigerate them in a tightly closed jar, they stay fresh for weeks.

_____

Add a small amount of lemon juice to your whipping cream and it will whip more quickly.

_____

Potato chips, corn chips, tortillas, nuts, and muffins all freeze well.

_____

If you've got too much frosting left over after you've iced the cake, spread the leftovers between two graham crackers and freeze for dessert treats.

_____

When onions are in season, nice and sweet, buy extra. They will last a month or so. Keep in a dry, cool place.

_____

For sweet, fresh pineapple, simply prop the pineapple upside down on its head for 24 hours before cutting. This allows the juices and natural sugar to saturate the entire pineapple.

_____

Never slice your onion to make soup; just peel and put the whole onion in to make a sweeter pot.

_____

An easier way than a rotation system to remember which

eggs are fresher is to purchase white eggs one week and brown eggs the next.

————

Make weekly menu plans. This way you can utilize market specials and save time and money.

————

During the summer, when green peppers are at a good price, buy a large supply, chop them up and freeze in self-sealing plastic bags or small jars. They are ready to use for pizza, hamburgers, meat loaf, and salads.

————

To shape meatballs, use an ice-cream scoop, or shape into a round log and cut off slices, then roll into balls.

————

Avoid putting foods on radiators, in warm automobiles, or on sunlit windowsills. Heat will spoil the food.

————

Keep a supply of dry milk on hand to use when you run short of fresh milk or need a small amount for a recipe.

————

Put one lug of cucumbers in washing machine and wash in cold water ten minutes—spin—rinse—spin (one full wash cycle). Remove cucumbers, rinse in cold water at the sink. Your cucumbers are ready for the jars.

————

Instead of pouring salad dressing over salad, spray it on.

Fill one clean spray bottle with one part vegetable oil and three parts wine vinegar. Spray on greens.

————

Here's a list of some of the basics you should have when cooking:

- liquid measuring cups—a 2-cup measure will handle many jobs
- dry measuring cups—these usually come in nested sets from ¼ to 1 cup
- measuring spoons—these also come in sets which include ¼ teaspoon, ½ teaspoon, 1 teaspoon, and 1 tablespoon
- wooden spoons and large metal spoons
- rubber spatulas—at least one
- shredder—one with fine holes
- timer
- tongs
- colander—for draining
- rolling pin

The rule is to buy the best saucepans you can afford. A good strong pan with a riveted handle and thick bottom will last a lifetime. It's nice to have 1-quart, 2-quart, and 3-quart saucepans. But if you can only choose one, select a good 2-quart saucepan.

Other basics include:

- Dutch oven
- skillet
- baking pans
- wire racks
- electric mixer
- knives—a good knife is worth its weight in gold. It can make cooking tasks much easier and save time.

Emilie's Bran Muffin Recipe

Ingredients Needed:

Raw bran

Chopped dates, raisins
  and/or apples

Oil

Honey

Molasses

Eggs

1 quart buttermilk

Baking soda

Salt

Wheat flour

Raw coconut

Walnuts

Crushed pineapple
  optional

FIRST MIXTURE (in a regular-size bowl):
1½ cups dates, raisins, and/or apples; 2 cups boiling water; and 2 cups raw bran. Mix together.

SECOND MIXTURE (in a very large bowl):
1 cup oil (optional); 2¼ cups honey; ¼ cup molasses, and 4 eggs. Beat together.

ADD TO SECOND MIXTURE, THE FOLLOWING:
5 cups wheat flour; 5 tsp. baking soda; 1 tsp. salt; 5 cups raw bran; 1 quart buttermilk (a little bit at a time).

ADD FIRST MIXTURE TO SECOND MIXTURE, then add walnuts and raw coconut. Optional: Add 1 can crushed pineapple, drained.

Bake at 375° for 20-25 minutes. Fill muffin tins two-thirds full. Batter can be stored for up to 2 weeks in an airtight container in your refrigerator. Muffins can be frozen after they are baked.

❦

Don't shop for groceries
when you are hungry.

Kitchen

Gidgets & gadgets

$\mathcal{S}$he watches carefully all that goes on throughout her household, and is never lazy.

(Proverbs 31:27)

Place the plastic lids from coffee cans under bottles of cooking oil to keep cabinets clean. When the lids get dirty, just throw them away.

A rubber jar opener (or rubber gloves) gives you easy access to anything in a tightly closed jar.

To cover kitchen cabinet shelves, I apply easy-to-install vinyl floor squares by just peeling off the backing. They are particularly good for lower shelves where pots and pans are usually stored. They cut easily and do not tear or wrinkle.

One of the best appliances I have for my busy schedule is my crockpot. I prepare the meal early in the morning and when I come home from shopping or work, I find our main dish for dinner ready.

At least once a year pull the plug on your refrigerator and give it a thorough cleaning. Rinse with clean water after cleaning with baking soda (one tablespoon baking soda to one quart water). Let it air dry.

A trash can under the kitchen sink takes up some very valuable storage space. We take a large decorative basket and line it with a plastic bag. The bag is easy to lift out when full. Train several family members to help take the trash out.

Glue a 12-inch square of cork to the inside of the cabinet door over your kitchen work area. On the cork tack the recipe card you are using and newspaper clippings of recipes you plan to try within a few days. It keeps them at eye level and they stay spatter-free.

When using your electric can opener, help save your fingers from cuts by placing a refrigerator magnet on top of the can before opening it. This magnet will give you a good grip when you lift off the lid.

Increase your efficiency with an extra-long phone cord that will reach to all corners of your kitchen. Instead of wasting time while on the phone, you can cook, set the table, or clean out a drawer. A speaker phone provides similar freedom.

Meat slices easier if it's partially frozen.

Want to mix frozen juice in a hurry without using the blender? Use your potato masher on the concentrate.

You can peel garlic cloves faster if you mash them lightly with the side of the blade of a chef's knife.

To keep bugs out of your flour canister, put a stick of spearmint gum in the flour and it will be bug free.

I mark my bowls and their covers with the same number, using a marking pencil. Then I'm not always looking for a matching cover for the bowl when I'm putting away leftovers. All I have to do is match the numbers.

Arrange your kitchen for maximum efficiency. Position often-used utensils in convenient drawers and cupboards. Make your dishes do double duty. Use a saucepan as a mixing bowl; then use the same pan for the cooking.

Cut the lid off an egg carton and place the cups in a kitchen drawer. You can then organize your cup hooks, small nails, paper clips, thumbtacks, and other small items. No more junky drawers.

When you are in need of extra ice cubes for party or summer use, simply fill your egg cartons with water and freeze.

To find spices quickly, put spices on a double-decker lazy Susan. When storing your spices, simply alphabetize them on the racks: the top layer can be A-K, the bottom L-Z. Then when your family members or guests are looking for a specific spice, it will be easy to find.

If wax has built up on the felt pads of your floor polisher, place the pads between several thicknesses of paper toweling and press with a warm iron. The towels will quickly absorb the old wax.

For a quick shine between waxings, mop with a piece of waxed paper under your mop. The dirt will also stick to the waxed paper.

To avoid a smelly garbage disposal, run cold water and the disposal at the same time for a while with each use of the disposal.

To speed up a sluggish drain, first run hot tap water down the drain, then pour in three tablespoons of baking soda and one-half cup of distilled white vinegar. Stop up the drain and wait 15 minutes. The baking soda and vinegar will foam up, reacting with each other, and will eat away at whatever is slowing the drain. Finally, flush the drain with hot tap water.

Have fresh lemon juice all year long. Squeeze lemons and freeze juice in ice cube trays. Transfer the frozen cubes into freezer bags. Defrost for fresh lemon juice any time.

Use pressure cookers, microwaves, or electric pans or ovens when you can. They use less energy than your stove or oven.

Do not store cookies, cereal, or other "bait" by the stove. Children can get burned climbing on the stove to reach an item overhead.

Use glass or ceramic pans for baking; you can reduce your oven temperature by 25° F.

Instead of using the dry cycle on your dishwasher, open the machine and pull out the top shelf just an inch or so to prop the door slightly open. The escaping steam helps to dry the dishes almost as well as the dry cycle, it's much faster, and it saves energy and money.

I've found an easy way to clean the grater: Before using it, spray with no-stick vegetable spray.

Want spotless dishes whenever you use the dishwasher? Then be careful at the supermarket. Shake the box of dishwasher detergent; it should sound loose and powdery. Old, lumpy detergent won't do the job properly.

Line the bottom of the sink with a towel when you wash your precious glassware or fragile ceramic plates.

When you are defrosting the refrigerator, put an old bath mat in front of the fridge. It will help catch spills.

A great way to repair those nicks on your kitchen cabinets: Go over the nicks with a marker that matches the finish of the cabinets. You can polish over them with clear fingernail polish.

To renew shine and clean the top of toaster or toaster

oven, simply heat appliance and wipe with damp dishcloth. It will clean and shine fast.

———

Never refrigerate those pale, off-season tomatoes. Let them ripen on the kitchen counter until ready to eat. Refrigeration kills the taste.

———

Put a decorative hook by the sink. Hang your watch and rings on it while you work.

———

To absorb any leftover moisture from your lettuce container, put three or four paper towels on top of lettuce and seal bowl. Invert bowl and store in refrigerator upside down. Each time you remove lettuce during the week, replace paper towels.

———

Always bring water to a boil in a covered pan.

———

Cook as many foods in the oven as you can at one time to save money on the electric bill.

———

Match the size of the pan to the heating element so more heat will get to the pan.

———

Keep a small plastic shaker bottle filled with baking soda

with your dishwashing supplies. It is handy to take a stain out of a coffee cup or polish chrome-finished small appliances while you wash dishes without getting the soda box soggy with damp hands. Be sure to clearly label the bottle.

The one-dozen size egg carton fits perfectly in the bottom of a large grocery sack. When tea bags, coffee grounds, and juicy wet items are thrown away, the carton absorbs the liquid and prevents dripping trash bags across the carpet or linoleum.

Keep gasoline and other flammable liquids stored in closed containers and away from heat, sparks, and children.

When postage stamps are stuck together, place them in the freezer. They will usually come apart and the glue will still be usable.

If you have a gas stove, make sure the pilot light is burning efficiently with a blue flame. A yellowish flame needs adjustment.

Cook with a clock or timer; don't open the oven door continually to check food.

Purchase a large, plastic lazy Susan to store cleaning

items under the kitchen sink. I also use lazy Susans in the linen closets, sewing room, baby's room, office, and refrigerator. They are also great to use under bathroom sinks for shampoos, hair spray, creams, etc. The same large size lazy Susan can also be used for pots and pans.

Rather than making the first day of school a time to dread, I decorate the kitchen with crepe paper, make a special breakfast, and leave new pencils at each child's place setting.

When preparing fruits and vegetables, lay an old newspaper on your counter to catch the peelings. Don't lay the peeled vegetables on the newspaper. When you are finished, just roll up the paper and throw it out, or add the vegetable waste to your compost pile.

Wash utensils and dishes (if possible) as you go. Also wipe the counter as you go. It will save time in the long run.

Add cold water immediately to pans, dishes, and utensils that were exposed to raw eggs, hot milk, and cooked cereal or other sticky starches.

Reusable containers that held milk or juice should be rinsed as soon as they are empty. If they get smelly, refresh them by soaking them in a mixture of water and one tablespoon of baking soda.

To reduce odors and stains on countertops, coat the cutting surface with vegetable-oil spray before cutting up onions or berries.

———

To keep your SOS pad from rusting, place it in something airtight. The pad will last much longer. Make sure to put the lid on tight. Also try placing the airtight container in the freezer.

———

A nutcracker is a great twist-on bottle cap opener. It unscrews the caps with ease.

———

My mother always took time to make single things extra special. I have happy memories of asking for an orange and then delighting to see she had cut it into a lovely basket shape and filled it with fruit. This made me feel special and loved.

———

Leftover linoleum can be cut with scissors into placemats any size you like.

———

Keep a cupful or two of wheat germ or bran in a screwtop jar near your breakfast center or cooking area. Replenish it from the large supply stored in your freezer.

———

To remove burned or baked-on foods from your cookware,

scrub with baking soda sprinkled on a plastic scouring pad, rinse, then dry. Or let a warm paste of this solution soak on the burned area (keep wet); then scrub as needed.

Liquids for soups, stews, or hot drinks should be collected whenever you drain cooked vegetables.

To eliminate unpleasant cooking odors, boil one tablespoon of white vinegar in one cup of water on the stove.

Use Scotch-brand hair set tape (pink roll) to label freezer items. You can write on the tape with a felt-tip pen. It lasts a long time.

To really clean your white porcelain sink, give it a bleach bath. Fill the sink with about two inches of water and add one-half cup of chlorine bleach. Wait 15 minutes. Then rub the bleach solution all over the porcelain and rinse thoroughly.

Recipes accumulate so easily. I use a small ($5^{1}/_{2}$ x $8^{1}/_{2}$) three-ring notebook and organize according to topic, labeling the notebook in the same way. At the beginning of each category, I add an envelope (punched so that it is attached) and keep small recipes in it until I have time to fill a notebook page.

Want an easy way to keep your drains clear? Flush them with boiling water every so often.

To remove heel marks on your linoleum, wipe the spots with kerosene and turpentine.

Here's a way to keep trash cans fresh and presentable. Buy the cheaper plastic trash can liners in a roll. Open the first bag and, leaving it attached, drop the whole roll in the trash receptacle, turning the top of the open bag over the trash can (now the roll is under the open bag). When it is full, grasp the sides together, lift with one hand, and tear it off the roll with the other hand. After closing the used bag for disposal, open the next one, leaving it attached to the roll. No more scrounging for bags.

If your white appliances have been scratched, you can dab some white typewriter correction fluid over the scratches, let it dry, and then apply an appliance polish over it.

Put a product called Iron Out in a soap container in your empty dishwasher. Wash using the complete cycle. If the dishwasher is extra stained or dirty, repeat a second time. Your dishwasher will come out spotless. (Iron Out can be purchased at a hardware store.)

Before I use a new cast-iron frying pan, I like to season it. First, I wash it with warm water and thoroughly dry it. Next, I put the pan on a burner until it's very hot, add a few tablespoons of oil, and swirl it around the pan. (Peanut oil is especially good because it doesn't burn.) Then I pour out the oil, let the pan cool, and repeat the process. Now the pan has been properly seasoned and food won't stick.

———

Take your empty plastic vegetable bags from the market, fold lengthwise in fourths and roll over a toilet paper tube, securing with a rubber band. They store neatly in a drawer and are ready to use anytime.

———

Deodorize your refrigerator with one opened box of baking soda. Place it in the back of the refrigerator or in a shelf on the door. Change every other month.

———

Cheese that you plan to grate for pasta dishes and casseroles can be cut into chunks to fit in a lidded quart jar. You can store it in the refrigerator almost indefinitely without the cheese spoiling.

———

Freshen drains and garbage disposal with the discarded box of baking soda previously used in your refrigerator.

———

See-through jars and plastic containers are great for storing kitchen items such as tea bags, sugar, flour, beans, noodles, rice, oatmeal, popcorn, cookies, and raisins. They keep fresh and are easy to spot.

———

Cover shoe boxes in wallpaper or contact paper and put

your packaged food mixes, such as taco mix, gravy mix, and salad dressing mix in them.

Save time by labeling pantry shelves with a labeler or stick-on labels to indicate food items such as soups, canned fruits, cereals, canned veggies, or baking items.

Washing walls? You'll work better, feel less strain in your arms if you vary your movements, alternating a series of vertical strokes with horizontal or diagonal ones.

When burned-on food crust in a glass pot is a problem, fill it with vinegar and water and boil for 20 minutes. After that, scrape away softened crust with a plastic scouring pad.

❦

The Lord didn't burden us with work.
He blessed us with it.

Cleaning

No more
sticky streaks

*I*n everything you do, put God first, and he will direct you and crown your efforts with success.

(Proverbs 3:6)

To keep a bowl steady when whipping or mixing ingredients, place it on a wet, folded cloth.

———————

To prevent lime buildup at the bottom of teapots, put a marble in the bottom. As it rolls around, it keeps the lime from building up.

———————

To keep your closets smelling fresh and clean, use a box of scented fabric softener sheets. Open the box and set it on a shelf. Close the door and each time you open it, you get a pleasant whiff of fragrance.

———————

Nail polish remover takes off price tag stickum just great.

———————

Ever wonder when to use sudsy ammonia and when to use clear? One manufacturer explains that the sudsy product cuts through tough grease and grime quickly, but may leave streaks on shiny materials. The clear formula is preferable for use on glass, stainless steel, chrome, and other shiny surfaces.

———————

Cleaning up the shower mat: When the shower mat begins to look grungy, it's time to soak it in a tub full of warm water and distilled white vinegar. Then give the mat a good scrubbing with a stiff bristle brush, rinsing thoroughly.

———————

A good way to keep stainless steel range hoods clean is to

pour undiluted liquid dishwashing detergent onto a damp sponge and thoroughly clean the grease off the hood. Rinse with a clean, damp sponge, then dry the hood with a clean, soft cloth. Afterward, go over the surface with a spray protectant usually used to protect vinyls in cars. Wipe a small amount of the protectant over the stainless steel, polish with a soft cloth until the metal shines. Then every day or so, wipe off the hood with a DRY cloth. Repeat the application of the protectant every few weeks or as needed.

———————

Need a great cleaner for those extra-hard-to-clean clothes, ones that are stained with blood, grass, ink, grease, paint, or dirt? Use multipurpose Goop hand cleaner with a toothbrush. You might have to go over the spot more than once. It does clean.

———————

When using a sink full of hot water to rinse the dishes, add a capful of vinegar to cut any excess grease or soap. This will give your dishes a clean, sparkling look.

———————

If you have work to do around the house while there is something baking in the oven, put a timer in your apron pocket so it will alert you when it's time to take your food out of the oven.

———————

An easy way to remove price tags from vases and dishes is to put two to three drops of cooking oil on the tag and rub it a bit. It comes right off.

———————

To keep silverware tarnish free, put a piece of blackboard chalk in its box.

After sweeping the garage and hosing it down, I use a squeegee (the kind on a long pole that is used for windows) to "pull" the water out. The floor is soon dry enough to replace all the items.

———

You can clean glass on your pictures without leaving smudge and smear marks by dusting the glass well and then polishing with tissues designed to clean eyeglasses.

———

Use Windex spray to shine scuffed patent leather shoes. Just take a clean cloth and wipe clean.

———

Put a sachet in the bag of your electric broom so the room will smell fresh and sweet after you sweep it.

———

Having tried everything to remove adhesive left by the decals that slip-proof the tub, I found the solution by accident. My drain had backed up, so I poured liquid drain cleaner into the tub. After the solution drained, I began to wipe out the tub and found that the glue came right off.

———

Plain baking soda is an excellent cleaning compound. Wet your finger or a piece of paper towel in water and then dip in the soda and rub it on stubborn stains.

———

I found it very difficult to remove lime deposits around

my sink fixtures until I discovered that a paper towel (or two) saturated with white vinegar and wrapped around the fixtures removes this buildup of lime.

Next time you want to paint something with oil-base paint, choose paint thinner (mineral spirits) instead of turpentine for wiping up smudges and cleaning brushes. Paint thinner costs less and its smell isn't as heavy as "turp's."

Don't throw out barely-used paper napkins. Retrieve them and keep them with cleaning supplies. They make thrifty and handy paper towel substitutes.

To prevent soap buildup, cut a sponge to fit soap dish above sink. After using soap, place soap on sponge, not soapdish. Makes for easy cleaning later.

Don't throw away empty two-quart detergent bottles, especially the ones with the built-in measuring cup. Wash them thoroughly and use them to make fine watering containers for your household plants.

Pregnant ladies or elderly people can clean their bathtubs easily by using a mop. Saves the bending.

Gum can be removed from fabric, hair, and so forth, by

using lighter fluid on a piece of cotton. Rub gently and it comes off easily. Don't use around fire or heat.

————

Instead of opening and closing the refrigerator door several times a meal, I put everything on a counter next to the refrigerator. Then I open the door once to put things into the fridge.

————

After becoming extremely frustrated with tub and tile spray cleaners, I decided to try an easier way to clean the tile around my tub. I filled my plastic plant watering can with laundry detergent, liquid bleach, and hot water, and "watered" the tile around the tub with it. Almost instantly the tile became bright and shiny—even before I began to scrub!

————

When cleaning the glass doors on our fireplace, I use a standard window cleaner on the glass for the easy-to-remove grime. Where the soot is baked on, I dip a damp paper towel into the fine wood ash on the floor of the fireplace. When this mixture is rubbed over the burned-on stains—presto! Off they come with no ill effects to the door's transparency.

————

For those hard to reach places around the bathroom faucet, use a toothbrush. It gives a nice shine too!

————

For washing windows inside and out, measure two gallons

of the hottest water your hands can bear into a pail. Add two measuring tablespoons of cooking cornstarch and stir well. This solution can be used until it cools. (This sounds like a lot of water changes, but you can do many windows before cooling occurs.) On the outside, use newspapers to dry the windows. This works very well.

To clean silver, in your hardware store purchase a product called "whiting." Add ammonia or alcohol, making a paste. Apply over silver with a damp cloth, rinse in hot water, and wipe dry. For cleaning the hard-to-get-at crevices, simply use a soft, old toothbrush.

For those nasty stains in your toilet bowl, use a pumice stone (can be purchased at a beauty supply shop or drugstore). Rub the pumice stone over stain in toilet bowl and, presto . . . the stain comes off. Be sure to clean under the inside rim of the bowl too.

To prevent the nozzle on a can of spray paint from becoming clogged, turn the can upside down after each use and depress the spray head until the air is clear of paint. We do this in our paint shop, and we never have any problems with stopped-up sprayers. It clears the tip so it won't clog.

Those beautiful cut glass vases, bowls, and glasses will sparkle if you wash them in soapsuds and one tablespoon of bluing.

To remove water spots from your shower tile and glass

doors, use nonsteel wool. Rub scrubbers on the walls while they are dry and then wipe them down with a damp towel.

Place a nylon stocking over your dust mop. Throw it away after using and you can keep your dust mop clean.

To remove the odor of garlic or onions from your hands, pour a little white vinegar in the palm of your hands and rub together.

Some refrigerator energy-saving tips: Clean off the coils in the back or bottom of the refrigerator every other month to improve efficiency. Locate the refrigerator away from heat-producing appliances such as an oven or dishwasher. Check the tightness of the door seal. If any part of the rubber gasket on the inside of the door is loose, brittle, or cracked, replace it. Don't overfill or underfill the compartments. Arrange items so cold air can circulate evenly.

If your summer ice chest has a musty smell, just add six charcoal briquettes and close the lid for a few days. The smell will disappear. Charcoal also takes the musty smell out of a damp basement.

To clean those yucky glass shower doors, take a small pail and add 1½ cups of blue fabric softener. Do not dilute. Using a sponge, go up and down the door, over and over. Do not rinse. Let it air dry and all the yuck will be gone.

A cover-up apron with two large pockets is great to wear on housecleaning days. I can go from room to room and use one of the pockets for pick-ups and the other pocket to hold my dust cloth. Just remember to empty the pockets before washing the apron.

If you are painting and you need to stop for a while or even overnight, put your paintbrush in a big plastic bag, squeeze the air out, put a rubber band around the handle, and put in your freezer. It will come out and soften up, and you can start painting right away.

To clean windows and mirrors with no streaks, wipe off cleaner with newspaper instead of paper towels.

Rub floor scratches away with fine steel wool dipped in floor wax.

For a grass stain, use liquid detergent and sponge the area. If the spot is stubborn, apply rubbing alcohol, rinse, and wash. Use bleach if the fabric allows.

Water rings or hot dish rings can be removed by making

a thick paste of equal portions of salad oil and salt. Rub it on the spot with your fingers and let it absorb for a couple of hours. Then rub it off with a soft cloth.

———

Scorch that beautiful linen cloth? Simply rub the scorched area with a raw onion, soak in cold water for a couple of hours, and then wash the linen as usual.

———

Mop or rub varnished woodwork or floors with cold tea.

———

To clean mini-blinds, remove from the window and put into a bathtub of warm, sudsy water. Slosh them around, rinse, and rehang. If they are too large for the tub, take them outside, hose off, clean with a soft brush or sponge and liquid detergent, rinse, drip dry, and rehang. To maintain, use a feather duster on your mini-blinds weekly. They should only need major cleaning annually.

———

To polish copper, mix vinegar with salt and you will have beautiful, shining copper.

———

Proper paintbrush maintenance: Always clean the brush as soon as you finish a job, except on big jobs that take more than one day. You can soak brushes overnight in water or thinner until the next day's use. Remember, the better the tool, the better the job.

———

For cleaning those hard-to-get-to places, I keep a baby

bottle nipple brush alongside my other scrubbers. It's especially great for quickly cleaning cheese graters.

No more rusty scouring pads and a job for your children: When you get home from the market, hand them the box of pads and a pair of scissors, instructing them to cut the pads in half. You usually only use one-half pad per job.

To remove lipstick, liquid makeup, or mascara from fabrics, soak in dry-cleaning solution and let dry. Rinse and then wash.

For ballpoint pen ink stains, put a towel under the stain and blot the spot with rubbing alcohol. Moving the towel to a cleaner section, continue to blot until the spot is removed. Then wash as usual.

For mildew stains: Wash in bleach if the fabric is safe to use bleach on; or rub the spot with lemon juice and salt, let it dry in the sun, and then wash as usual; or scrape off the mildew and sponge it with alcohol and a mild detergent.

❧

Don't put it down, put it away.

Laundry

Make wash day
a winner

Fear not, for I am with you. Do not be dismayed. I am your God. I will strengthen you; I will help you; I will uphold you with my victorious right hand.

(Isaiah 41:10)

If you are tired of your box of laundry soap taking up so much room, you can take an old canister and fill it up with your favorite soap and you will have more room.

I wash all my panty hose at one time by putting them in a pillowcase, folding the open end over, and fastening it with a safety pin. I put the pillowcase in the washing machine with other delicate items. I then place the pillowcase in the dryer on a low heat.

A great way to freshen and fluff pillows is to throw them into the dryer and run them through without heat (just air) for a few minutes. The tumbling will get rid of the dust and freshen pillows at the same time.

To dry a bulky sweater faster and safer, place it between two fluffy bath towels and roll lightly with a rolling pin. Then remove the sweater and put a hand towel inside it before flattening and shaping it to dry. The hand towel absorbs still more moisture.

When washing panel curtains, wash them in Woolite in cold water and it won't be necessary to press them.

When your iron sticks, just sprinkle a little salt onto a piece of waxed paper and run the hot iron over it. Rough, sticky spots will disappear as if by magic.

Always wash your throw rugs in cool or lukewarm water.

Hot water will cause the rubber backing to peel. Let the rug dry on a line instead of in the dryer. You can fluff it up when it is dry in the no-heat cycle of your dryer.

———

If your children manage to get holes in their clothes almost as soon as they get them, try this: Use fleecy bathrobe velour to patch your children's clothes. It is inexpensive, 100 percent synthetic, less plushy, and comes in many colors. It wears very well.

———

To get stains out of colored polyester clothes: Presoak in one-fourth cup automatic dishwashing detergent to one gallon hot water for several hours. Then launder as usual.

———

When I want to wash a rug that sheds, I put it in a pillowcase (an old one that I keep just for that) and tie the top well. Then I have no mess in the washer. Just shake out the pillowcase.

———

To make old curtains look like new, rinse them in a sink filled with warm water and three-fourths cup of Epsom salts after washing. Let soak for 15 minutes, rinse in cold water, and hang curtains on the line to dry.

———

To remove wrinkles from anything plastic around your household, such as tablecloths, shower curtains, or shelf paper, use your hand-held blow dryer.

———

Here's a little trick to make ironing easier. Using pieces

of wax candles in an old cotton sock, swipe your iron every so often while ironing. The wax makes it glide smoothly, and ironing goes faster.

———

As you sprinkle your clothes for ironing, sort them. Separate those materials needing a high, medium, or low temperature. This will save you from having to root through the basket as you iron.

———

When you notice a missing button or a tear while you are ironing, do not put those articles away until they are fixed. Mend them promptly.

———

If starch sticks to the bottom of your iron, scour it with steel wool. Never scratch it off with a knife or a razor blade.

———

When ironing double thickness—collars, cuffs, hems or pockets—iron on the wrong side first and then on the right side for a much smoother finish.

———

Ironing boards never seem to have enough padding. When the pad on your ironing board is ready to be thrown out, leave the pad on the board. Just add your new pad and cover the old.

———

Taking proper care of your comforter will keep it looking

like new. Check the care label before tossing your comforter into the washing machine. In general, all polyester-filled comforters and most down-filled comforters are washable. Comforters filled with wool should be dry-cleaned. Although a certain filling might be washable, some cover materials, like satin, would be ruined if washed. Dry-clean instead. When washing your comforter, set the machine on the gentle cycle. Drying on the lowest heat setting will prevent filling from shifting.

———

A great "closet organizer" for socks, scarves, mittens, and swimsuits is a cardboard juice carton with dividers. Take off the top lid; cover the box with colored decorative adhesive paper. Place the box on its side on a wardrobe shelf and you have some great cubbyholes for those little items. Also keep a similar box in your laundry room so each rag has its own cubbyhole.

———

Metal zippers work more smoothly when you occasionally rub the teeth with a bit of wax or bar of soap.

———

When machine-washing sweaters, place them in a pillowcase to keep them from matting and insure that they retain their shape and fluffiness. Sweaters will last longer too.

———

To freshen laundry, add one-third cup baking soda to the wash or rinse cycle. Clothes will smell sweeter and cleaner.

———

Putting clothes away: If you could use more help sorting

and returning clean clothes to their owner, put a shelf in the laundry room. Set plastic dishpans on it and label each pan with a family member's name. On wash day each person can collect his own clothing.

Stack towels, washcloths, and linens with the folded edge toward you. This makes it easy to pick up one at a time when you reach for them on the shelf.

I'm always dropping socks, underwear, and combs between my washer and dryer where I can't reach. I solved my problem by placing a narrow piece of carpet on the floor between the two appliances. When something falls, I pull out the strip and the article comes with it.

Instead of using expensive fabric-softener sheets, pour one-fourth cup *white* vinegar in last rinse of the washing cycle. This eliminates static cling, helps remove wrinkles, gives clothes a fresh smell by removing soap, and cleans the drains of the washer by removing soap scum and lint.

In cold weather, wipe your clothesline with a cloth moistened with vinegar to prevent your laundry from sticking to the line. Wax the line once a month to keep black marks off your clothes.

Wet shoes can dry quickly without increasing the electric bill. Place shoes with inside or top of shoe facing the exhaust side of the refrigerator.

To stop a run, use hair spray or clear nail polish.

───────────

When you wash curtain panels, use a laundry marking pen to mark each drapery as you take it down to indicate which window it belongs on. After cleaning the draperies, you will not have to guess which panel goes on which side of what window.

───────────

Dampen a washcloth with liquid fabric softener and toss it in the dryer with your clothes. It works well and is much cheaper than commercial softener sheets.

───────────

Always wash knitwear inside out, either by hand or machine, to avoid snags.

───────────

Never iron permanent press shirts again. After washing, simply throw two shirts into the dryer for eight to ten minutes. Hang on hangers immediately.

───────────

Keep the crinkles crisp in seersucker by adding a small amount of starch to the rinse water when laundering. The fabric will look fresher.

───────────

Use small safety pins to pin socks together in laundry. Weight keeps socks from clinging to other laundry and saves time in matching socks when folding laundry.

When wringing water out of corduroys, velveteens, or woolens, gently squeeze fabric and lay it on heavy towels, shaping it to the original size of the garment.

An easy way to sort laundry: Get three bags. One is for colored clothes. This bag should have lots of colors on it. One is for dark clothes. This bag should be navy, brown, or black. One is for white clothes. This should be a white bag. A king-size pillowcase works very well.

I am always surprised at how many people don't know it is incorrect to first put clothes in the washing machine and then add the detergent. The detergent should be added to the water and allowed to mix well before the clothes are added. In a concentrated form, detergent is strong and could harm fibers in fabrics.

I have tried reusing fabric-softener sheets in the dryer but could never remember how many times I had used them. I finally hit on the idea of tearing off a small corner each time I put a sheet in the dryer.

Protect all woolens, furs, and winter clothes during the summer months by cleaning and storing them in a mothproof bag or chest.

Don't overload your machine. This turns out a poor wash.

Keep in stock six or seven bobbins of the colors of thread you use most. This eliminates filling bobbins all the time.

A cloth dipped in two percent peroxide and used as a pressing cloth will remove most scorches.

———————

Hang your clothes outside in the fresh air and sun as often as possible. Germs meet a quick death, and the clothes smell wonderfully fresh.

———————

Iron dark cottons, rayons, and woolens on the back of the fabric to avoid shine marks from the iron.

———————

A neat way to use liquid laundry detergents on "ring-around-the-collar" is to pour a small amount of detergent into a cup and use a small paintbrush or toothbrush to apply it to the collar. This eliminates waste and helps you get the detergent where you want it.

———————

When your panty hose are new, take them out of the package, wet them thoroughly, and put into a plastic bag and freeze. They will last longer, saving you money. I also have heard that to resist runs, they should be lightly starched.

———————

To remove garment wrinkles: Hang wrinkled garments on the curtain rod in your bathroom and run very hot water from the shower. Close the bathroom door and let the water run for a couple of minutes. The steam will fade the wrinkles from your clothing. Great for those who travel.

Keep hangers handy and hang the clothes, as they are ironed, on a rod nearby.

———————

To make your blankets fluffier, add two cups of white vinegar to a washer tub of rinse water.

———————

If you forget to remove clothes from the dryer, simply wet a washcloth or hand towel, throw it in the dryer with the clothes, reset dryer for ten minutes, and wrinkles are gone.

———————

Fold towels lengthwise, then double. They will be ready to place on racks. If folded widthwise, they will need to be opened and refolded.

———————

To clean the lint filter out of the washer or dryer, use a hair pick. It works great, especially if the lint is wet.

———————

Launder your blankets in the summer and store them for winter in clean paper sealed with gummed tape.

———————

If you like to keep your ironing board set up for quick touch-ups, buy a twin-size bed sheet that matches the color of the room in which you iron. Use the old cover as a pattern and make a new cover from the sheet. It will look nice in almost any room.

Keep a bottle of your spray cologne in the laundry room. When clothes, sweaters, or blazers smell like cooking or cigarette smoke, give a quick spray and place in the dryer on the air cycle for 10 to 15 minutes.

———

Hang a whisk broom on a hook beneath your ironing board. Use it to remove lint when pressing clothes.

———

To keep the outside metal part of your iron shining, dampen a paper towel and apply a small amount of toothpaste. Make sure your iron is cool. Wipe it clean with another paper towel.

———

White vinegar will remove permanent creases when rehemming pants or skirts. Simply dampen with vinegar and press with a warm iron. Repeat if necessary.

———

Use warm water to sprinkle your clothes. It penetrates them better. Allow clothes to absorb the moisture at least three hours before ironing.

———

If your steam iron clogs up, fill it with a mixture of one-fourth cup of vinegar and one cup of water and let it stand overnight. Heat the iron the next day. Remove the mixture and rinse with clear water.

❧

Plan your work, then work your plan.

Storage

Don't
be a coward.
Get rid
of that clutter.

*B*e beautiful inside, in your hearts, with the lasting charm of a gentle and quiet spirit which is so precious to God.

(1 Peter 3:4)

One of the worst results of a fire is the loss of family photographs. My sister keeps all her film negatives in her bank safe-deposit box. In the unfortunate event of a fire, she can have pictures reprinted and save precious memories.

Rather than keep bed linen in the bathroom linen closet and lingerie in bureau drawers, reverse it. It is so much easier because linen is then available in the bedroom and lingerie is right at hand to slip into after you shower.

Save empty cardboard rollers from toilet tissue for storing electrical extension cords or strings of Christmas tree lights.

I use old tin muffin pans as a divider system in my kitchen desk drawer. I love them. They hold those many small items I keep in my desk, such as paper clips, rubber bands, stamps, and address labels.

We all use cardboard boxes for storage and moving, but they are clumsy to pick up and carry. Take a knife and cut a half circle in each end or side of the box. These openings will serve as handles and the box will be much easier to manage.

Organize various kinds of plastic bags by wadding and tucking them into cardboard rolls from paper towels. You can label the tube with the kind of bag in each; small, produce, freezer, and so forth.

In packing my dishes for moving, I found that paper plates were perfect to sandwich between plates to cushion them. The smaller ones worked for dessert plates or saucers. With just a little newspaper between the stacks, they were ready to go.

Use half-gallon milk cartons as storage containers for freezing. Use whole for large amounts, or cut down to size for smaller amounts. Seal with wide, two-inch masking tape.

I usually purchase three or four types of cereal. Once a package is opened, it is very difficult to reseal it. I transfer my cereal to an extra large, self-sealing plastic bag. This keeps my cereal fresh and crisp down to the last bite.

To organize photos, make subject dividers out of 4 x 6 cards. Organize the photos by subject. For example: Henry, Margaret, vacation, animals, home. Then file in a shoe box.

When storing valuables, clothing, ski equipment, papers, photo albums, and slides (or any item), simply number your storage boxes and record the contents on 3 x 5 cards you file in a recipe-type box. This prevents a mess on the outside of the box. Also, if a burglar breaks into the house, he can't easily read the contents of each box and pick out what he wants. Color code them according to priority, such as red for the highest priority, so you can quickly pull these and get them out of your house in the event of a fire or flood.

———

A new thought for lining drawers and cupboards: Instead of putting the contact paper down on the bare wood, first measure the area to be covered and then cut a piece of cardboard, poster board, or mat board to fit. Then cover the board. Slip the covered board into the drawer or onto the shelf. Easy to cover, easy to remove for cleaning, and when or if you move, you can take them with you! Easy to use every scrap of contact paper too. No waste.

———

Cover apple-type storage boxes with calico fabrics and use for storage in bedrooms and closets. They look cute and are still very practical.

———

Use leftover wallpaper for shelving in pantry, cupboards, linen closets, and kitchen shelves. The paper gives new life to old, drab shelving.

———

A tightly lidded jar is also an excellent keeper for homegrown herbs that you've dried, especially mint and oregano. Sprinkle some of the leaves on green salads or use them to flavor sauces, soups, and stews. Make a cup of fragrant mint tea whenever you need a pick-me-up.

Store out-of-season clothes in large, plastic-lidded trash cans. Not only will your clothes be mothproof, they will stay dry in damp basements.

————

Here's a little trick to prevent tightened caps and lids of containers from getting stuck. Coat the rims of the containers with petroleum jelly before tightening the caps or lids. Works great on latex paint cans, tubes of artists' paint, nail polish bottles, and especially glue containers.

————

Buy several colored clothespins and keep them in the kitchen to use instead of those awful little wire "twist-ems" on bread sacks, cookies, and potato chips. They are much faster, easier, and keep items airtight.

————

My mother-in-law came up with a great idea. She stores her things in apple-type boxes, piling them three high. She went to the lumber yard and had a 24-inch round plywood tabletop made, set it on the boxes, and covered it with an adorable cloth that reaches to the floor. With a lamp on top, she now has end tables with storage underneath.

————

Leather handbags store well if stuffed with tissue. Wrap in tissue—never plastic—and place in a storage box or fabric bag. Plastic will dry out leather.

————

Work better and faster by tossing out things that are no

longer needed or have lost their usefulness, such as stacks of old magazines or receipts. If you don't want to throw them out, store them in a box. A good rule: Throw something away every day.

Insert paper plates or paper napkins between fine china plates as you stack them to prevent scratching.

I saved our family photos in a storage box over the years. Then one day I got some albums and put together a "This Is Your Life" album for each of the children from birth to college. I gave it to them as a Christmas gift. They absolutely loved it and cherish it to this day.

Store small children's socks in the bottom halves of plastic egg cartons. Put the egg cartons into drawers and use as dividers.

When mailing cookies, pack in popped popcorn or Styrofoam popcorn to help keep them from crumbling.

Egg cartons serve as excellent storage containers for jewelry.

Place a piece of chalk in your jewelry box to prevent costume jewelry from tarnishing.

To prevent moth damage, be sure to mothproof wools and wool blends, especially during summer months. Don't forget your sweaters. Use tissue paper to prevent clothing from coming into contact with mothproofers.

———————

Use fabric shoe bags or wrap shoes in tissue and put into shoe boxes.

———————

You've seen picnic-type baskets that have places to hold tall bottles. Put your tall rolls of gift-wrap in the places for the bottles, and put the ribbon, scissors, and tape in the picnic basket space. You can even set them out as a decoration.

———————

To store sweaters so they keep wrinkle-free, simply lay the sweater front side down and fold in half so the bottom meets the top, then cross each arm over the width.

———————

Before putting coats and boots away when winter's over, wax their zippers with a candle. The zippers won't be stuck or hard to pull up next year.

———————

If you store clothes and other items in boxes on high shelves, put a finger hole in the front of the box near the bottom. It's great for sliding the box off the shelf.

———————

One woman wrote, "Because we do not have room in our

home for an 'office' and I do not use my hall linen closet for towels (I store them in the bathroom cabinets), I was able to empty two shelves in the linen closet, which is next to our telephone station, and utilize them for an office." One shelf holds the notebooks, boxes with cancelled checks, a metal file box with pink slips, insurance policies and other important documents, and a cutlery tray for scissors, ruler, stapler, paper clips, and miscellaneous office needs. The second shelf has three cardboard file boxes without lids. They have folders containing personal files (paid and unpaid bills, correspondence, and tax records in the first box; articles by category which did not require a notebook because there were not that many of them in the second box; and teaching aids, transcription of notes taken at seminars, and information regarding community involvement in the third box). The office is very convenient, and the doors of the closet conceal it when it is not being used.

Go through old, saved magazines periodically. Tear out articles you wish to save. Staple the articles together, placing a three-hole punch on all pages. Using old three-ring binders (recover with contact paper), separate articles according to subject, put in binders, and label binders with label maker. Topics: home gardening, houseplants, decorating, home projects (building and remodeling), sewing, crocheting, knitting, miscellaneous, crafts, bazaar projects, Christmas ideas, toys, baby items (to name a few). You may need hole reinforcements because magazine pages are thin, or you can file the articles in file folders and label.

❧

Throw one item away every day!

Children

Lov'em, hug'em,
and kiss'em

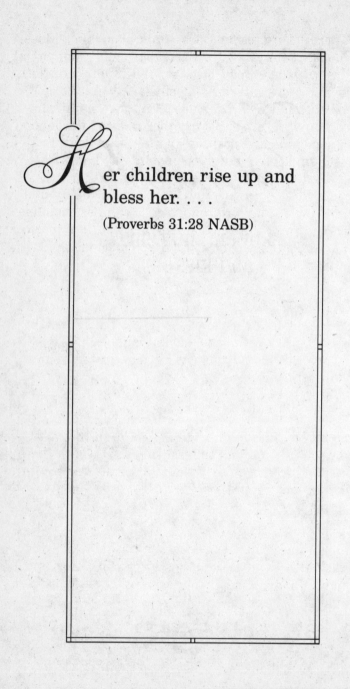

*H*er children rise up and bless her. . . .

(Proverbs 31:28 NASB)

Five Powerful Minutes for Dads—Talk about the values or psychology behind a television program or commercial you've just watched. Body, arm, or even thumb wrestle your child to a draw. Write a brief thank-you note of appreciation and encouragement to another significant adult in your child's life. Sit together in some uncommon place or some unusual position and see what conversation develops. Stop for five minutes on your way home from work to mentally adjust and prepare yourself for "reentry." Select a conversation topic to focus on around the dinner table. Play two rounds of "squiggles," a game in which one person draws a simple scribble on a piece of paper and the other person must then add lines that make it into something.

Have your kids used their crayons to decorate your painted walls? Try baking soda on a damp sponge to remove their murals. With a little elbow grease, your walls will look as good as new.

Instead of a bedtime story, I tell my children the beginning of a dream and suggest they listen with their eyes closed. They are quickly sound asleep and ready to finish the dream.

When plush toys that aren't machine washable get dirty, spray with dry shampoo, let stand for ten minutes, and brush out with a soft-bristled brush. Refluff the fur with a portable hair dryer set on low.

When we are dining out, these ideas help keep our

children busy until the food comes: 1. Before ordering, have everyone look at the menu, point to the pictures of food and name them, count the sandwiches or desserts, say the prices aloud. Make a list of favorite foods.
2. After deciding what to order, count how many napkins, straws, utensils you will need. Play "guess what's under the napkin" or "pick up the straws." 3. Have everyone close his or her eyes and identify various sounds: people talking, a baby crying, a clock ticking, feet moving along the floor, dishes rattling. 4. Tell an add-on story: One person starts it and each one adds another sentence until your meal arrives.

———————

Once a year, I have a baby-sitter swap party. Each attendee must bring the names and telephone numbers of three reliable sitters.

———————

A tasty variation on the standard peanut butter and jelly sandwich: Make sandwich as usual, but just before serving, butter outside of bread, and brown sandwich in a hot skillet.

———————

One most-appreciated gift a neighbor gave me after the birth of my first baby was a freshly baked apple pie with a card attached worth eight hours of free baby-sitting. The pie hit the spot, since I was tired of eating all that hospital food, and it was reassuring to know there was someone available close by to baby-sit if needed.

———————

When sewing buttons on children's clothing, use elastic

thread. It makes buttoning much simpler for little fingers.

———————

After many nights of interrupted sleep, I finally hit on a solution that keeps my five-year-old in her own bed—at least most nights. I labeled one bowl "Mama's Bed Buttons" and another "Christine's Bed Buttons" and put 25 small buttons in each. For every night Christine stays in bed, I owe her one button. She pays me a button if she gets in bed with me. When her bowl is filled, we do something special—a roller-skating trip, a movie, an outing of her choice. Now she only comes to my bed if she really feels she has to.

———————

Here is a little idea for young children at a fast-food store or restaurant. When you buy the tot a soft drink, cut the straw off short so it is easier to hold and drink. Less chance of a child spilling or dropping the drink too.

———————

As a mother and nurse, I know how uneasy and scared children can become over appointments with a doctor. When the need arose for my two-year-old son to be treated at an emergency center, I brought his favorite stuffed monkey along. Since my son was being treated for an eye injury, I had the doctor examine the monkey's eye first, then listen to the monkey's heart. When my son saw the doctor trying to help his monkey, much of his own fear was alleviated.

———————

Before bed, have your family prepare everything they

need for the next morning and put it on or next to the kitchen table to avoid a frantic search before you leave the house.

———————

Use a pair of adult socks as mittens for infants or small children; they are impossible for children to remove.

———————

To keep several kids' socks straight, assign each child a different color of sock sorters. After washing and drying, distribute socks to the owner of the appropriate color of sorters.

———————

Put a laundry basket in each child's room. Have each deliver it full to the laundry room and sort the wash. Children who are tall enough to reach into the bottom of the washer can be taught how to run it.

———————

I have books from childhood that I cherish deeply. To keep them childproof, I have taken the time to cover each page (and the front and back covers) with clear contact paper. Your child's favorite books can be protected the same way for years to come. A low-cost heirloom.

———————

When I empty the dishwasher after dinner, I wrap a flatware place setting in a napkin for each family member. This way, the children are able to help set the table, and the job gets done faster.

———————

Television should be off unless eyes are on it. Programs

should be selected from the TV schedule with regard to their value, interest, and plot.

———

Use children's flat bed sheets of Spiderman, Peanuts, and so forth, as party tablecloths. If so desired, spread clear vinyl over them to protect from soiling.

———

My son loves to play with his snap-together building set, but come bedtime, he doesn't like picking up the many, many pieces. Solution: We lay out a large sheet for him to play on. When he has to go to sleep, we whisk the floor clear in a jiffy by gathering up the sheet and storing it with all the toy pieces inside till the next time he wants to build something.

———

To help children remember the proper way to set the table, tell them that "fork" and "left" both have four letters, while "knife," "spoon," and "right" all have five letters.

———

Children who grow up in environments full of put-downs, negative nicknames, and criticism often become critical adults. Catch your child doing something good and tell him about it. Be positive and uplifting.

———

The most powerful forms of praise are given in private, one-on-one.

———

The more we do for our children, the less they can do for

themselves. The dependent child of today is destined to become the dependent parent of tomorrow.

––––––

The greatest gifts that parents can give their children are the roots of responsibility and the wings of independence.

––––––

My husband and I write the date, occasion, and age of our children on a standard-size piece of white typing paper to correctly and permanently date the home movies we make of them. I put the paper on the floor and my husband takes a shot of it before we begin videotaping the kids. We also date each new section of unused tape before continuing to shoot with the same roll.

––––––

The happiest, best-adjusted individuals in their present and older lives are those who believe they have a strong measure of control over their lives.

––––––

I don't buy children's books. I make them with family photographs; typing paper; clear, self-adhesive paper; scissors; paste; and watercolor markers. I cut up the photos, using just the face or sometimes the whole person, and paste them on typing paper. Next, I use markers to draw in an imaginative background—placing a picture of my child on a cloud, for example, or on a turtle, or on a rocket going to the moon—and write a few descriptive words. I cover each page, front and back, with protective self-adhesive paper, put all the pages together, and staple them. The books are cleanable and personalized, and my children love them!

When my children were small and I made a pie for dinner, I would use the extra pie dough by forming a ball and rolling it out on a greased cookie sheet. I would sprinkle cinnamon and sugar on it, bake it for ten minutes, then cut it into squares.

———

To stimulate my toddler's interest in good dental hygiene, I buy trial-size tubes of toothpaste. These tiny tubes are easy for her small hands to manage, and because they contain her special toothpaste, she enjoys brushing her teeth more.

———

Sometimes young children won't take their medicine from droppers or spoons. A useful idea is to take a clean nipple from one of their bottles and measure the medicine into it. The child will suck the medicine very naturally.

———

I have three children who like to stay outside in the early evening and play together. When I need to call them in for the night, I just turn on my front porch and outdoor lights. That way I don't need to yell all over the neighborhood, and they know it's time to come in. You might have to adopt the flashing method to catch the eye of your child.

———

As a parent, I never wanted my children to make a mess on the floor under the high chair when we went out to a restaurant. I always brought an old newspaper to the restaurant. I would spread the newspaper under the high chair and, after the meal, would fold it up with the mess intact and ask the waitress to dispose of it. It makes things a lot neater for the next group.

———

I have a great hint for mothers with babies. I know it's hard to pour out baby oil! You either get too much, or it spills. I've figured out a convenient way to put on baby oil. Take an empty roll-on bottle (you can get the ball off with a metal nail file), wash it out well, pour the baby oil into the bottle, and replace the ball. The oil will glide on smoothly and won't make a mess.

———

Let preschoolers make use of an egg timer to give each of them and their friends a chance to play with a toy. This will add to their fun during playtime. It will help prevent unnecessary quarreling also.

———

Many times it is hard to read the ounce measurements on baby bottles, so I paint them with red nail polish.

———

When only half of the jar of baby food is used, simply refrigerate. The next day, if it seems watery, add a small amount of dry baby cereal to thicken.

———

Teaching small children to make beds can be easy. Simply use a fitted bottom sheet and a comforter. If the comforter has stripes, it will be easy to throw on the bed and keep the stripes in line with the edge of the bed. A top sheet is not especially necessary with today's beautiful comforters.

Comforters are fast, and easy for you and your children to handle.

Let your baby hear you pray for him. He will gradually come to know the wonderful Person you are talking to, the One who cares about him.

A good way to help your older child celebrate the arrival of a new baby is to have the child share the news with his friends. On a paper bag, write "It's a boy!" or "It's a girl!" and the name of the new arrival. Inside the bag, place lollipops tied with blue or pink ribbons. The child can take the bag and pass out the candy so everyone can share in the excitement of the new baby.

The wedding anniversary of our friends was approaching, and my husband and I desperately tried to think of a gift. Since our two families both have a preschooler and kindergartner, we decided to give them a weekend away from their children. The four kids loved spending the weekend together, and the celebrating couple loved their blissful solitude. For our anniversary, they offered the same arrangement.

My husband and I have a four-month-old son. We have started a tape cassette of different things we want to remember, which one day he and his children will enjoy. We have taped crying spells, first cooings, even the noisy way he sucks his pacifier. This is something that will be cherished for many, many years and it adds a new dimension to the "memory album." Another idea is to plan a photo album with pictures of the baby, then record his sounds on those picture-taking days. Date the snapshots and the cassette, and you'll have his precious photos along with a sound track.

According to the most recent studies on drug abuse among teenagers and young adults, there are three cornerstones in the lives of those young individuals who do not use drugs of any kind: religious beliefs, family and extended family relationships, and high self-esteem.

Reward children for household chores. If they do not complete the job and have already received their allowance, then have the child reward you for completing his or her work by paying you back some of the allowance.

Tape pictures of socks, T-shirts, and so forth, on dresser drawers in your young children's rooms. They then will know where everything goes when putting their clothing away.

Here's a way to make a great cool drink for your child. Put his or her favorite flavor pudding in a blender, adding twice the needed amount of milk. Blend for a few seconds. It tastes like a thick, frosty milkshake. You could also add some ice cream. It's low in calories.

If I pin my children's socks to their outfits, it saves time and eases the frustration of having to dress them in outfits with socks that don't match.

––––––––––

When my children get bored (holidays), I send them on a scavenger hunt—either inside the house or out in the yard. My list includes easy and hard things, i.e., a small bug or ant, a dead leaf, a red button, and so forth.

––––––––––

When my children are riding in the car on a travel trip, they make up games to amuse themselves. One of their favorites is "I'm looking for. . . ." The object can be anything—a red truck, a blue blouse, a pine tree. The first child to see the object picks the next one.

––––––––––

A great way to use hand-me-downs is to take the white clothes and dye them pink or blue, depending upon the sex of the new child. If the new child is a girl, you can spruce up the old clothes by adding appliques, ribbons, or lace to make them look frillier.

––––––––––

Keep children busy during dinner preparation with a glob of shaving cream on the counter or high chair tray. They will love finger playing with it. Since it is soap they will only taste it once. It is also fun for them to play with in the bathtub. This introduces them to different textures. You can also use toothpaste, whipping cream, or clay.

––––––––––

If your baby is cutting teeth, take a baby bottle nipple

and fill it with water and freeze it. When it is frozen, put it back on the bottle and give it to your baby. This numbs his gums and, as the ice melts, the water goes back into the bottle so he will sleep more peacefully.

Just another hint for that bothersome junk mail. Save it and give it to the little ones when they are bored. They love to open mail, especially mail containing colorful coupons or stickers. If it is just an ordinary letter, the back usually is plain, so they can draw or write on it and reseal it in the envelope included. If you have no small ones, give the mail to someone who has.

Save your old magazines. Use the pictures in the magazines to help the children learn to read.

Add a little club soda to pancake mix for light, airy pancakes.

If you have teenage children who are involved in many different activities, try this: Purchase several duffle bags on sale (three to four dollars). Fill them with the supplies needed for each activity (special shoes, racket and balls, helmets, suntan lotion for the beach). Keep the bags filled and ready to go in the hall closet.

Decorate your child's room by having him draw pictures of his favorite activities on butcher paper, making a mural, and putting it on the walls around the room.

One mother of several children found that she was always discussing who left the towel, comb, toothbrush, cereal bowl, hair dryer, or beach chairs lying out. She solved this by having each child choose his or her own color. Then as she could afford to, she purchased all the items in each child's color. For company, they chose a set of green towels which was always kept clean and hanging on the rack. The family loved and appreciated the new game system.

———

Divide children's toys into three separate boxes and rotate the boxes each week to avoid boredom with playthings.

———

Pick-up bags: Use felt markers or crayons to decorate a grocery bag for picking up items at the end of the day. The children go from room to room picking up their toys, shoes, clothes, or whatever. If there is nothing left in any room, they get a sticker on a weekly chart. If they have three stickers at the end of the week, they get a sheet of stickers for their collections. If they have five stickers in one week, they get two sheets of stickers. If there is anything not picked up, the child it belongs to gets no sticker for that day.

———

Assign a designated place where each child can study, and a regular time to do his homework. Make sure there is plenty of light, ventilation, and quietness.

———

Keeping your child or children busy while you are visiting or just don't have time for them is a hard task.

Ask your butcher for the end of a roll of butcher paper (or obtain end rolls of newsprint from your local newspaper). Let the children color it, paint it, finger paint, or draw on it. Then roll it up again and store it. At Christmas, use this paper for gift wrapping. The children will be thrilled to see their artwork displayed.

———————

Never pay children for doing something for themselves; it actually robs them of self-esteem and is a form of bribery.

———————

Let your young child play within your sight in the kitchen. Talk, sing, and play together. Have one shelf for the things the child is allowed to use. If you have a small kitchen, keep these toys or pots and pans in a separate box in the garage.

———————

No matter how well organized I was, my children always seemed to leave for school forgetting something. Plastic dishpans (a different color for each child) were my solution. Into them I put lunch boxes, books, notes to the teacher, homework, and the like. A quick glance tells young students whether or not everything is in the bin.

———————

I make each one of my boys an ornament to hang on the Christmas tree. My first one was a ceramic cherub with the year lettered in gold. This year I am going to crochet the ornaments, and every year I will make something a little different, dating each one.

✿

Children need strength to lean on,
a shoulder to cry on,
and an example to learn from.

Safety

First—precaution
Second—aid

*H*ow precious it is, Lord,
to realize that you
are thinking about
me constantly!

(Psalm 139:17)

You can take certain precautions when staying in hotels or motels while traveling. Take a travel burglar alarm that can be hung on the doorknob at night. Push a chair under the doorknob to help prevent the door from being opened. When leaving your room, put the "do not disturb" sign on the outside of the door and leave the TV on at low volume. Don't leave valuables in the room. Check them in the office safe.

Keep firearms under lock and key where there are small children. Teach older children how to handle them safely.

Keep your stairways from becoming a hazard. Remove articles lying on the steps.

Put side rails on small children's beds to keep the children from falling out.

In the attic and basement, paint the top and bottom steps white as a precaution against stumbling.

Make sure your fireplace is equipped with a metal fire screen to prevent sparks from flying out on the carpet.

Keep a plastic carry container filled with basic first-aid supplies like cotton balls, adhesive tape, bandages, sharp scissors, sterile gauze, antiseptic, and tweezers. Keep this handy to take outside or on a picnic.

Keep a coffee can full of baking soda near your stove in case of a grease fire.

Dispose of smoking materials carefully (not in waste-baskets), and keep large, safe ashtrays wherever people smoke.

Don't cook over open flames wearing long sleeves or a flowing night robe or gown.

Rubber mats can become slippery and are not always skid proof. Once a week turn your mat over and clean with a cleanser, scrubbing off the film. Rinse well.

If someone is caught on a high-voltage electric wire, throw the main switch or break the contact with a dry piece of wood (such as a wooden broom handle). In no way touch the victim until he is freed from the current.

Your bathroom can be a dangerous place for a little one. A few simple measures go a long way in helping to prevent accidents: Keep on hand only those medicines that you use regularly, and store all medicines out of children's reach. Lower your water heater thermostat so curious little hands won't get scalded by turning on the hot water faucet. Never leave an appliance plugged in around water. Drape a towel over the top of the bathroom door to keep children from locking themselves in. A strip of tape across the doorknob bolt will also work. Stick nonslip appliques or strips to the bottom of the bathtub to help prevent falls.

Keep toilet tissue on a shelf or in a cabinet instead of on the roll. While not dangerous, toilet tissue fascinates small children, who might stuff the entire roll down the toilet and clog pipes.

When giving a child a pill, raise his head. If he is lying flat on his back when he takes the medicine, it may go down his windpipe instead of into his stomach.

Never touch an electric appliance or plug with wet hands. Warn your children of this hazard.

Always turn the handles of pots and pans away from the edge of your stove or counter. You will avoid catching them unexpectedly and spilling the contents over yourself or your child.

To plan a fire escape route for your home: List all possible exits from your home, as well as two from each bedroom.

Be sure everybody can reach and operate latches, locks, doors, and chains. Tell your children that they can break a window in case of fire. Instruct them to remove large fragments of glass and cover the sill with a blanket. Draw a floor plan of your home. Include windows and outside features like trees. Mark primary and secondary exits from each room. Designate a meeting place outside of your house where the family will congregate. Mark it on the map. Go over the plan with every family member and walk through the various escape routes from each room. Make sure children understand that they can't hide from a fire but can escape it by following an exit route. Conduct fire drills every six months. With each drill, vary the location of the imaginary fire and instruct family members to alter their escape routes accordingly.

Never spray liquid insecticides near electrical outlets or exposed connections. Short circuits may result.

Always load sharp knives into the dishwasher with the blades down.

Burn yourself? Apply raw egg white to the burn—quick relief and helps the healing process.

All chemicals and medicines in your home are potential poisons and should be kept away from children.

Remember, never squirt lighter fluid into hot barbecue

coals, as the flame could be drawn up the stream, causing the fluid to explode.

Never leave poisons in an unmarked container or a soft drink bottle. Clearly mark all poisons and indicate the proper antidote.

Don't call medicine "candy." Your youngster might like it so much he will take it on his own when you aren't looking. This can result in severe illness or even death.

Place gates at the top and bottom of your stairways when youngsters are small.

During the warm summer months seat-belt straps can be uncomfortable because we wear thinner clothes. I find that if I wrap a handkerchief or piece of terrycloth around the strap where it will touch my neck, I can wear the seat belt with comfort and be safe too.

Keep knives, scissors, plastic bags, ice picks, and matches away from the reach of children.

Post the telephone numbers of your fire department, family doctor, police, and the office of a working parent in a conspicuous place where every family member can find them immediately if needed.

Never leave a room with a candle burning near curtains, drapes, or combustible decorations.

Keep your basement, closets, garage, and yard cleared of combustibles like papers, cartons, old furniture, and oil-soaked rags.

Keep a round rubber gripper designed to open jars close at hand to use when grabbing the rod to pull yourself up out of the bathtub. It keeps your hands from slipping, possibly preventing an accident.

When using water softeners, bath oils, or bath salts, be careful not to add too much, especially if you don't use a mat at the bottom of your tub. The added products will soften the water, making the tub very slippery, which could cause a fall.

When glass breaks in the sink or on the floor, simply wet a paper towel or napkin and wipe up all those little slivers. The slivers will stick to the paper and you will avoid cutting your fingers and feet.

❧

A house is made of walls and beams;
A home is built with love and dreams.

Beauty

Looking &
feeling great

*C*harm can be deceptive and beauty doesn't last, but a woman who fears and reverences God shall be greatly praised.

(Proverbs 31:30)

I have found a good home recipe to condition hair: Apply mayonnaise, which contains such conditioners as eggs, soybean oil, and lemon juice, to damp, newly washed hair. Rinse off thoroughly with warm water.

———————

When my feet are tired, I place them in a basin full of warm water with two tablespoons of baking soda or Epsom salts and let them soak for 20 minutes.

———————

A great mask for oily skin: Make a paste of one unbeaten egg white, a half cup of pure lemon juice, and a half cup of oatmeal. Apply to face and let dry completely. Rinse well with warm water.

———————

To help me relax during my last few months of pregnancy, I make this all-natural recipe for my bath water: Add two tablespoons of lavender flowers, three tablespoons of bay leaves, four tablespoons of oatmeal, and four tablespoons of bran to a pot of water. Simmer for one hour. Strain and add to bathwater.

———————

Incorrect shaving of legs can cause rashes and irritations. The right way to shave is to moisten legs with warm water, apply shave cream, and wait three minutes to allow hair to become soft and pliant. Using a fresh, sharp blade, shave in the direction of hair growth for sleek, bump-free skin.

———————

I have oily skin on my nose, chin, and forehead and dry

skin everywhere else. To take care of my skin I: 1. Wash with a mild foaming gel to cleanse without overdrying. 2. Sweep some alcohol-free toner over my face with a cotton ball to remove any lingering oil and dirt. 3. Dab oil-free moisturizer on dry areas.

———————

It is always better to arrive for any function looking our best. A first step in good communication is good appearance. It is a way to make a favorable first impression on people who are important to us until we can project our inner selves through conversation.

———————

While you are supervising a child's evening bath, give yourself a facial, pluck your eyebrows, or do your pre-bed beauty routine.

———————

A good way to clean out the fragrance when you change perfume in your atomizer is to wash the atomizer well with soap and hot water, fill the bottle with rubbing alcohol, and leave it open overnight.

———————

To dry your fingernail polish, spray your nails with Pam (no-stick cooking spray).

———————

After having a good cry, my eyes are swollen. I soak cotton balls in cool skim milk, then place them on my closed eyes for five to ten minutes.

———————

Three simple steps for a facial at home: 1. Wash your face

as usual but don't follow with toner or moisturizer.
2. Boil some water and pour it into a large mixing bowl. Create a steam "tent" by draping a large bath towel over your head and the bowl, keeping your face about six inches from the hot water. Steam face five to eight minutes. Steaming softens skin and opens pores. 3. Deep clean your face with a grainy cleanser. You can use a commercial scrub or make one by mixing one teaspoon each of oatmeal, honey, cornmeal, and plain yogurt. Gently massage over face and neck. Rinse thoroughly with warm water and pat dry.

If you're tired of spending money on powder puffs, you can make your own. First buy your favorite powder, then get a container. Fill the container with cotton balls. Pour some powder in and shake. Now, whenever you need to powder, just grab a cotton ball.

When I exercised I quickly became bored with the 1-2-3 counting of every exercise. Now I count backwards (instead of 1 to 50, I count 50 to 1). Doing those grueling exercises doesn't seem to take as long when I'm concentrating on counting backwards.

More than 90 percent of skin cancers occur on body parts exposed to the sun's radiation. Protect your skin with a good sunscreen when outdoors (a lotion with a SPF value of 15).

Once a perfume or cologne is opened, its "life clock"

145

starts ticking. You can prolong the strength of any fragrance by following this advice: Refrigerate a fragrance or keep it cool. Coolness slows the aging process. Purchase two small bottles rather than one large bottle to get greater strength and longevity. Make certain the fragrance has a tight cap. When transferring a fragrance from its original container to a collector's bottle, be sure to cleanse the new bottle first with alcohol.

———

Find a low-maintenance hairdo.

———

Take a shower at night, use electric rollers in the morning. You'll have plenty of hot water then and more A.M. time.

———

Throw out all makeup you seldom use. If green eye shadow hasn't looked right on you so far, it never will.

———

Keep all cosmetics you use every morning in one place— on a shelf, in a clear Lucite organizer, or plastic zippered bag—so you don't have to think about what to reach for. Keep duplicates in your purse or at work; don't waste time fishing for them when you are rushing to get ready.

———

Put on makeup and eat breakfast before you blow-dry your hair. Your hair will dry faster, stay healthier.

———

Stash emery boards and covered elastic bands in the kitchen, the car, and at work.

When you have rough elbows, you can make them smooth the following way: First massage elbows with a facial scrub, gently rubbing in a circular motion to lift off dead skin and smooth away roughness. Then, soak elbows for five minutes in a bowl containing half a cup of baby oil and half a cup of hot water. Repeat this gentle scrubbing and soaking process twice a week until your elbows are soft. Make time twice a day to smooth on your favorite rich body lotion. If your elbows are discolored as well as dry, try rubbing them with a cut lemon once or twice a week.

———

One of the best "no-cost" facials, which tightens your skin and makes it feel soft and refreshed at the same time, is created when you make an omelet (or anything that requires three or four eggs). Just scoop out the remaining egg white from each shell with your finger and spread it on your face and neck. Leave the egg white on for about 15 minutes, then wash it off with cool water. It's super.

———

Hair blower techniques: Concentrated blasts on a single section of hair do not do the job. This technique overheats the hair. You should move the current of air all over your hair, holding the dryer about six inches away from hair. Combing and drying against the natural growth direction of the hair keeps it from clinging to your head and gives a fuller look.

———

Cornstarch is a supersoothing dusting powder. To get more mileage from your store-bought dusting powder, just mix half and half.

———

Use lemon juice as an astringent, unless you have very

dry skin. Lemon juice has a drying effect. It also will whiten the skin. You can mix it with glycerine to make it less sharp.

To put life into dry hair, use olive, almond, or avocado oil as a conditioner. Warm the oil and saturate your hair; then wrap your head in a hot towel for 15 minutes, wash, and rinse well.

Spend this Saturday doing something you really want to do. I don't mean next month. This Saturday. Enjoy being alive and being able to do it. You deserve it. There will never be another you. This Saturday will be spent. Why not spend at least one day a week on you!

Take time out to ride your bike, build sand castles, fly a kite, smell a rose, walk in the woods, or go barefoot in the sand. We adults need to explore the wonderful world of the creative child within.

To take a stuck lid off of your fingernail polish jar, place in microwave for five to ten seconds. Top will come off easily.

When giving yourself a home permanent, protect your tender skin from chemical burn by applying a light film of petroleum jelly to the skin along your hairline and on the top and back of each ear.

———

How many calories can you burn in one minute of exercise (based on a 130-pound person)? Aerobic dancing—6.5; Bicycling—3.8 (5.5 mph) or 5.9 (9.4 mph); Golf—5.0; Hiking—6.6; Jogging—10.2 (6.5 mph); Rope skipping—7.5 (55/minute); Rowing machine—4.5; Riding—6.5; Stair climbing—6.7; Swimming—7.6; Tennis—6.4; Walking—4.5.

———

My favorite beauty aid is honey. I clean my face, put the honey on, relax for 10 to 15 minutes, and then rinse well. It's wonderful.

———

I save the scoops that come in coffee and powdered lemonade. I use them when I wash my hair. Rather than bringing bottles of shampoo and conditioner into the tub or shower, I simply fill one scoop with shampoo and one with conditioner and place them within easy reach on the shelf in my shower.

———

I could never find enough time to use my exercise bike until I thought of this—keep it by a telephone! You'd be surprised how much exercise can be done during phone conversations. Your hips will bless those long-winded phone callers.

———

Check your portable hair dryer for lint and hair buildup

on the air inlet screen. This buildup will cause the motor to get too hot and burn up. Make sure the hair dryer is unplugged.

❧

The most essential element
in any home is God.

Wardrobe

Save
time and money
with TLC

For I can do everything God asks me to with the help of Christ who gives me the strength and power.

(Philippians 4:13)

Take an inventory of your clothing. This will give you a visual look at what you have, what you need, what you must get.

Blouse and skirt/pant hangers efficiently utilize the space in a woman's closet.

To hang skirts, use wire hangers with clothespins clipped on.

To store scarves, belts, and small clutch bags, simply put them into clear plastic shoe boxes purchased at your favorite variety store.

When one leg in your panty hose gets a bad run, but the other is still okay, cut off the bad leg just below the panty part. Use it with another pair that has the same problem and you have saved a pair of panty hose.

After wearing leather shoes, let them air out overnight before placing in a shoe box and storing on the shelf. To maximize the use of your shoes, you need to rotate two or three pairs.

Hang blouses, skirts, and pants on the same rack so you can put together an outfit at a glance.

Keep your weekend clothes separate.

———

Make clothing repairs—loose buttons, torn hems—as soon as you take off a garment. At least don't place it in the closet until it is fixed.

———

When hanging clothes in a closet, place all hangers in the same direction. They will be easier to grab in a hurry.

———

Before wearing new leather boots, it is advisable to apply two coats of clear paste wax to protect the leather.

———

Hang wrinkled clothes in the bathroom while showering. The steam will cause the wrinkles to smooth out.

———

Skirts and pants are best hung on hangers with clips, or use clothespins on wire hangers.

———

Roll the family's T-shirts, socks, shorts, and panties, and put into their drawers. Family members can easily see what they need and find the right color in just one glance.

———

When I find a photo or illustration of a new use for an old

scarf, I cut it out and tape it on my closet door. That way I don't forget updated styles.

———————

If you think a pair of shoes are ruined, check with your shoe repairman before you get rid of them. Repairmen can often work magic. Our dog chewed on Bob's 125-dollar leather shoes. Our shoe repairman made them look like new and perfect for under ten dollars.

———————

Be sure to have your good leather shoes polished to retain the shine. It also "feeds" the leather, which preserves the shoes.

———————

Before storing wool blankets for the summer, wash them and add two cups of mothballs to the rinse water.

———————

Hang blazers and coats on padded hangers to avoid hanger marks at the shoulders.

———————

Even good jewelry can discolor your clothing, so dab the backs with clear nail polish. The polish can also be painted on jewelry with rough edges that could pull the fiber of fabrics.

———————

It is best to keep sweaters in a drawer or on a shelf rather than on a hanger.

To prevent garment damage, let your perfume or deodorant dry on your body before getting dressed.

———————

For sweet-smelling closets, hang an old nylon stocking filled with cedar chips in the closet. This also serves as an excellent moth repellent.

———————

Save store receipts, especially if you pay cash. This will save time later should you need to return an item. I tape my new shoe receipts on the inside lid of my shoe boxes.

———————

Don't clean one piece of an outfit and wash the other, or clean one piece and not the other. The colors may lose their match.

———————

Use hair clips to keep pleats in skirts. The pleats hold beautifully when the garments are packed in bags for travel.

———————

Keep makeup off your clothes by placing a scarf over your head before pulling garments on or off.

———————

You can machine-wash down-filled vests and jackets using a mild detergent and a gentle setting.

Replace heels and soles on your shoes before they wear down too much.

To prevent dampness in a closet, fill a coffee can with charcoal briquettes. Punch holes in the cover and place the container on the floor. For larger closets, use 2 or 3 one-pound coffee cans.

Don't shop when you are depressed. You may buy something thinking the purchase will pep you up. But you may be sorry later for the choice you made.

You can cut down on dampness in your closet by wrapping and tying together 12 pieces of chalk and hanging them in your closet.

An easy way to store off-season clothes is to use your empty luggage. Just add a bar of soap so the clothes won't have a musty smell. Store your luggage in a dry area.

Before putting on your panty hose, soften your hands with lotion. This will help cut down on runs caused by rough hands.

Rotate your clothing as much as possible. This will help

them regain their shape. Pick from the left and replace on the right.

———————

To remove spots from suede, use an art gum eraser.

———————

If shoes get wet, stuff them with paper towels and allow to dry away from heat.

———————

Shoe trees are great to keep the shape of your shoes.

———————

As soon as you take off your garments, empty the pockets, shake the garments well, and hang them up immediately.

———————

At today's cost, it's well worth it to take care of your shoes, using professional products often to protect them.

———————

Spray fabric shoes with Scotchguard to repel dirt. Treat leather shoes with a good polish.

———————

Brush suede shoes with a suede brush to bring up the nap. Rub off little spots with a nail file. Apply liquid suede cleaner only if necessary.

———————

Dry-clean garments every eight to ten wearings or longer if possible. Dry cleaning is hard on fabrics.

If panty hose are frozen (in the package) before being worn, they will last longer.

———

Keep good panty hose rolled and in the original envelope, or in a sandwich-size plastic bag. Ones with runs (to be worn under pants), fold double lengthwise and knot in the middle. Sure saves time when you're in a hurry to dress.

———

To stop static cling, simply run a wire coat hanger between your slip and dress. This draws out the cling.

———

When you remove your dress, turn it inside out and hang it carefully over a chair at the end of your bed. This helps rid it of perspiration and body odors.

———

For panty hose that are completely "shot," cut off the elastic (saving it for sewing) and use stocking part for stuffing craft projects, or cut the stocking in strips for tying plants to stakes.

———

Indisputably, cedar smells better than mothballs. What is debatable is the common notion that the aromatic wood protects clothing stored in cedar-lined closets and chests from snack-hungry moths. The secret to protecting belongings from moth damage is to have the clothes thoroughly cleaned before putting them away for the season in an airtight unit. Cleaning before storage will destroy any eggs or larvae that could otherwise develop and damage clothing. To restore the fresh scent of cedar, buff the wood lightly with fine sandpaper.

❧

Wisdom enables one to be thrifty
without being stingy,
and generous without being wasteful.

Sewing

When you give a darn

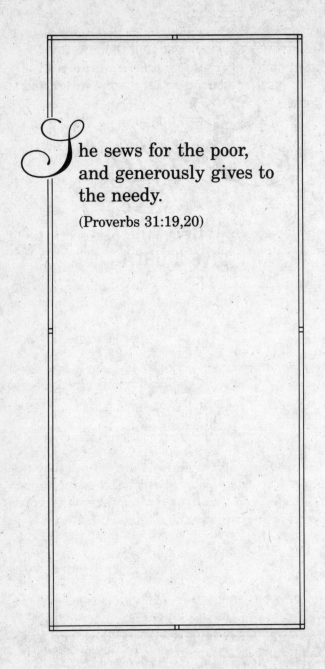

She sews for the poor,
and generously gives to
the needy.

(Proverbs 31:19,20)

If you have needlework patterns that become frayed because they are loose, try inserting them in 8 x 10 plastic refill pages for photo albums. You can read through the plastic, and the pattern won't tatter and tear.

———

Crochet together those scraps of yarn to make a unique spread or afghan.

———

I keep an old jar in the wastebasket by my sewing machine. The lid has a small hole and a slot in it. When I have a dull needle or break a needle, I put it in this jar. I also put old razor blades in this jar. When full, I dump the jar in the trash and eliminate possible injuries.

———

When sewing, drop scraps and threads into a grocery bag as you go. Don't let them clutter your machine and work area.

———

I keep an up-to-date list of all my fabrics posted by my sewing area. These are organized into seasons and garments. I always read this list over before going shopping. This helps me keep impulse buying of fabrics to a minimum.

———

A sewing trick I find very helpful is to cut out several dresses or items at one time and stack them by my sewing machine. Then I can sew them up when I have little bits and pieces of extra time.

When sewing, I stitch as much together as possible on a garment before I do any ironing. For example, I stitch the darts, pockets, and all other pieces I can sew without crossing a seam. I then iron it all and proceed.

When knitwear snags, pull the snag through to the wrong side of the garment using a fine crochet hook. Smooth the pulled threads as much as possible in the direction of the snag. If the pulled thread is long enough, tie it in a small knot. If the snag has caused a hole in the fabric, darn the hole.

An easy way to thread a needle is to spray some hair spray or spray starch on your finger and apply it to the end of the thread. The thread stiffens just enough to ease the job of guiding it through the eye.

Keep a small magnet in your sewing basket and use it to pick up pins and needles that drop to the floor while you are sewing.

You can reuse an old zipper by spraying it heavily with spray starch. It will sew in like new.

Here's a tip for keeping those four-hole buttons on longer: Sew through only two holes at a time, breaking the thread and knotting it for each pair of holes. This way, should one set break loose, the other side will still hold the button.

To make additional belt holes, poke belt with a red-hot steel knitting needle.

A bar of soap makes an ideal place to stick needles and pins. It lubricates them so they will go through stiff fabrics with ease.

Recycle your spotted T-shirts or blouses by decorating with stitchery or stencils. You can create your own designer garments.

Sewing together single or multicolored rug remnants is a task. But it does brighten up small areas of a room at low cost.

An easy way to hem a dress is to have a sink plunger handy to use when marking a skirt for hemming. Mark the handle at the desired length, then move the plunger around the hem. It stands by itself, leaving your hands free to mark or pin.

After oiling your sewing machine, stitch through a blotter several times to prevent surplus oil from damaging your fabrics.

You can sharpen a machine needle by stitching through a piece of sandpaper.

To solve the problem of finding the slit on the plastic spools of thread, keep a small magnifying glass close by.

I kept losing my crochet needles until my sister came up with a very good idea. She took half of an egg carton, turned it egg-cup up, and made holes large enough to fit each needle. I keep my thread, measuring tape, buttons, and scissors in the egg cups and don't lose my crochet needles anymore.

Use dental floss or elastic thread to sew buttons on children's clothing. The buttons will take a lot of wear before falling off.

To make your patterns last longer, spray a new pattern with fabric protectant. The pattern will last longer, rip less easily, and resist wrinkles.

Use a glass marble as a darning egg when mending fingers on a glove.

To make a straight cut for a buttonhole on heavy fabric, lay buttonhole section over a bar of soap and cut with a razor blade.

Add leather or suede patches to jacket elbows. You can

also add this fabric or fabric binding to worn jacket cuffs and the front of jacket openings.

———

Always wash all fabric before cutting to allow for shrinkage and for bleeding of colors. Use the same water temperature and drying method you will use for the finished garment.

———

Sew an extra button or two to a piece of fabric from a garment and store it in your button box for easy finding at replacement time.

———

Save handwork by using iron-on bonding material for hems in lightweight fabrics.

———

As the child grows, make notes on favorite patterns about larger and longer waists and arms.

———

Remove the back pocket on pants to patch holes in knees.

———

On generously cut garments, you may be able to position a dart or seam to "seam out" the problem.

———

Try tie-dyeing T-shirts that are badly stained.

———

I had put up new curtains but had never gotten around to

buying ties to hold them back. Wanting fresh air in my home on a warm, sunny day, I pulled off my multicolored plastic bangle bracelets and slipped each panel through one. It worked great—an inexpensive, easy way to drape curtains.

A wonderful idea for a holder for your crochet thread is to take an empty gallon jug, slit the side so you can put the ball of thread inside, pull the thread up through the top of the bottle, and then tape up the slit in the side. This method also keeps your thread clean.

Sew on shank buttons and metal overall buttons with dental floss to keep them from being torn off.

Use empty vitamin bottles or other small containers with childproof caps to store pins and other little sewing notions. Contents are easily visible, yet safe from children.

Cut too-short overalls apart at the waist and insert a wide band of matching or contrasting fabric.

Another use for used fabric-softener sheets—they make wonderfully strong interfacings in cuffs, pockets, and flaps.

Our family loves large towels. Many times I can't find

large enough ones in the stores, so I take two smaller ones and sew them together. The family is happy with their new large towels.

———————

Keep ribbons, elastic, lace, and the like in separate self-sealing bags. They are easy to find and do not get tangled in the drawer.

———————

If you want a matching quilt or bedspread and curtains, purchase sheets that match the quilt and make into valance and curtains. Pillow slips can be doubled to make tiebacks.

———————

Give a second chance to a dress. Cut it along the waist-line, turning it into a skirt. Add zipper, belt, buttons, or lace to give it a new look.

———————

Sew a sweater inside a coat as an extra liner.

———————

When making a tablecloth to be used on an outdoor table, put a triangular pocket across each corner. If the wind is blowing when you use the tablecloth, drop a rock in each corner pocket.

———————

Original eyeglass cases can be made out of purchased pot holders. Just fold in half and sew the short side and the long side.

When threading a needle, tie a knot in the end of the thread as you begin to pull it off the spool. This helps to keep the thread from tangling. Cut the thread from the spool at an angle. It is much easier to slip through the eye of the needle.

When counting rows in knitting or crocheting, tie a piece of different-colored yarn every tenth row. This will help you count easily, and the yarn can be pulled out easily.

When making clothing, dampen a toothbrush and rub across seams that keep opening before they are pressed.

Don't throw away those old curtain valances. Just cut the valance in half and sew the two pieces together to form the tiers of an apron. For a tie, slip ribbon through the valance casing. It's such a cute idea you may want to buy new valances (on sale, of course) and make these aprons as gifts.

Sharpen scissors by cutting through fine sandpaper a few times.

Time-saver for the seamstress: Make a short apron with pockets to hold pins, scissors, thread, and so forth. Then sew a measuring tape upside down across the bottom inseam. Everything you need is within an arm's reach when sitting at your machine, or ironing and measuring hems.

Sew plastic by placing a sheet of newspaper beneath it so it does not stick to the sewing machine.

Protect your fingers against needle cuts by coating your fingertips with a few layers of clear nail polish.

Soiled knitting needles can be cleaned by applying a light wax coating. This cleans and polishes the needles, and you can then work easily with the yarn.

Sheets make great wash-and-wear tablecloths and napkins. One king-size sheet makes one large cloth and 12 napkins or two smaller clothes and six napkins each. A twin sheet will fit most dining room tables perfectly without cutting or hemming. One yard of fabric will make six napkins when cut into 15-inch squares.

Grandma always had a tough time threading a needle, so she would dip the thread in clear nail polish. It dries quickly and threads quickly.

Spray knees, cuffs, and collars of small children's garments with fabric protectant. Spills and such will bead up, and dirt can be wiped off with a damp cloth.

Cut off floor-length dresses to make short ones for another year's wear.

Mend a torn mesh playpen with dental floss or fishing line. Both materials are strong and work well.

————

Sew squares of quilted material onto the knees of pants for crawling babies; they protect both pants and knees.

————

To make your own pin cushion, cover a ball of steel wool with some decorative material. Inserting needles and pins into this type of pad keeps them sharp.

————

An old bath towel folded and stitched to form a small "pillowcase" makes a perfect cover for a hot water bottle.

————

Use Velcro instead of buttons to attach overall straps to overall bibs.

————

When in a hurry to hem pants, simply use masking tape for a quick, temporary job.

❦

Do you look at your home as an extension of your personality and warmth or as an endless lifetime of drudgery?

Plants

Improving
your green thumb

Then God said, "Let the earth sprout vegetation, plants yielding seed, and fruit trees bearing fruit after their kind, with seed in them, on the earth"; and it was so.

(Genesis 1:11 NASB)

To repot a large tree, I placed it in a pail until I prepared the pot. I found it easy to move the plant about in this pail since the pail had a handle, so I left it in there. I put a few small holes in the bottom for drainage and placed it on a plastic plant tray to catch any water that might drain through.

Four tablespoons of dishwashing liquid in one gallon of water will get rid of red spider mites on your plants. Spray the plant weekly until there are no signs of the mites. I also had mold in the soil of some of my plants. I used a solution of one tablespoon of vinegar in two quarts of water, and watered weekly with the solution until all the mold was gone.

I'm not one who has great luck with indoor plants, but I have a little hint that helped mine grow. Rather than throw the water out every time I boil eggs, I let it cool down and water my plants with it.

Vase life for cut flowers is extended by filling the vase with warm water.

If you have hard water with high mineral content, you can increase the vase life of flowers by switching to distilled or purified water. Do not use softened water, since it contains salts.

A solution of one part lemon-lime soft drink (not diet

types) and two parts water provides proper acidity, a bactericide to reduce cloudiness of water, and sugar to "feed" flower buds so they open completely and give extended life to cut flowers.

———

Pick flowers in early morning before they are stressed by heat. Strip off foliage that will be below the waterline. Fill a broad bowl with water, and use sharp shears to cut about an inch off the bottom of each flower stem. While holding the stem under water, transfer the flower immediately to a vase filled with warm water or preservative solution.

———

When spring arrives I begin to get my soil ready for planting. These ideas have been of help to me: With a pitchfork or spade, dig down at least eight inches into the soil, lifting and turning it. Remove any debris such as stones and twigs. Besides bringing new soil to the surface, a deep spading buries weeds where they'll decompose, provides air for the soil, and loosens soil for better drainage. Check for moisture. Make a ball of freshly dug soil in your fist. It should crumble in your hand. If it sticks together, it's too soon to work the soil. Spread two to four inches of organic matter (such as peat moss, leaf mold, compost, or decomposed manure) over the soil and blend in thoroughly. Rake the soil to break up soil clumps so that plants will have a smooth bed for their roots. Select an all-purpose fertilizer such as 5-10-5 and work into the upper three to five inches of soil. Add two to three pounds per 100 square feet.

———

To make your ivy leaves look new and shiny, spread a

little mayonnaise on each leaf and you will have a very pretty, shiny ivy.

———

Try this florist's trick: Put small vases of spring flowers in the refrigerator overnight. Change water in the morning. Or try immersing flowers in cool water for several hours to freshen.

———

Water bushy plants with a bulb-type meat baster. It allows you to reach through leaves to deliver moisture to the soil, where you want it. Easier and neater than most watering cans.

———

When raking leaves on a windy day, dampen the leaves slightly with a fine spray from the garden hose. They will not blow all over the yard, will be easier to put into a trash bag or container, and more leaves can be stuffed into the bag.

———

After we water our houseplants, the saucers become full and sometimes overflow onto the floor. We solved this problem by using a turkey baster. As the water drains through, we draw up the excess into the baster and transfer it to another plant. This prevents a mess and protects the finish on the floor beneath the plants.

———

Ferns are a bit sensitive to chlorine in tap water, so let the water sit overnight before watering. This allows the chlorine to evaporate. Ferns also like to be misted.

Before you water your houseplants, poke three or four holes in the soil with the handle of a wooden spoon. This allows the water to soak the soil thoroughly.

———

Pep up and green up your plants with a shot of liquid castor oil. Water well. Within a few weeks you'll get new leaves and greener plants.

———

Set all your houseplants in saucers or shallow containers to catch the overflow when you water them. These are readily available in stores.

———

Misting plants in the evening prompts health, decreases bugs, and is a chore kids love.

———

For beautiful azaleas, simply add two tablespoons of vinegar to a quart of water and use occasionally around your plants. They love acidic soil.

———

Never use commercial soft water to water your plants. The salt used to soften the water will eventually kill your plants. The best rule is to use untreated water for all plants.

———

Going on vacation? Simply put all your houseplants in the bathtub with a few inches of water. They will drink the water as needed.

Equal parts of milk and water make a great solution for polishing leaves of both indoor and outdoor plants.

———

Here is a hint for using empty gallon milk jugs. Set a gallon milk jug full of water beside a plant in your garden. Punch a tiny pinhole in the bottom of the jug so the water seeps out slowly. This helps keep the ground moist until the next rain comes along. It also works great when you can't water every day.

———

To prevent flowers from wilting, cut the end of the stems with a long slanting slice, place stems in hot water for ten minutes, then put them quickly into deep, cold water with four ice cubes.

———

Dust plant leaves with a feather duster, or better yet, with your hair blower (set on the cool temperature). This method is also good for silk flowers and plant arrangements.

———

Eggshells crushed and spread around your plants will encourage growth.

———

To control the weeds and grass that grow between your walkways and cement walk areas, simply pour boiling water containing two to four tablespoons of salt over them.

———

Ferns love a tea party. Dump your leftover tea into your

fern pots. A used tea bag planted in their soil will also reap beautiful, healthy ferns.

For those plants that like an acidic soil, sprinkle your leftover coffee grounds around the plants.

For the organic grower, soap suds can be used as an insecticide. Spray generously.

Schedule your plant feedings (indoors and out) the first of every month. You'll never forget to do it, and your plants will reward you with renewed vigor and beauty.

I love to garden and have a large vegetable patch. There's always the problem of birds pecking and ruining the vegetables. I found a way to stop them. I take empty soda cans, the type that open by pulling a ring, and I take the tops off with a can opener. I put a string through the holes in the tops and tie the tops to wooden stakes placed crisscross around the garden. When the tops move slightly, they shimmer and shine and it frightens the birds. The tops don't get rusty, so you can use them year after year.

I reuse my plastic planting trays when I start my vegetable seedlings. Before using, I scrub them in soapy water to remove residual soil. After rinsing, I soak them for 30 minutes in a solution of one part laundry bleach to ten parts water. After a thorough rinsing the containers are ready to use.

————————

To avoid bruising tomato plant stems when staking, fasten them to stakes with strips of panty hose.

————————

Be kind to your knees when working in the garden. Use plastic meat trays as knee pads.

————————

Because grapes don't continue to ripen after they've been picked, leave them on the vine until the first light frost.

————————

Give newly potted plants a little less light for the first few days.

————————

Repot only when needed. Spring is the best time because it favors new growth.

————————

Melted snow contains minerals that make it good for watering your plants.

————————

Transform an old barbecue grill into a conversation piece by painting it, filling it with soil, and planting flowers or vines in it.

If the seeds you are planting should be set in rows, you can use a broom handle to form the trenches. Press the broom handle into the dirt—about one-quarter inch deep—with your foot. You'll have a perfect row at the right depth.

———

Plant onions next to beets and carrots to keep bugs away.

———

If you plant basil near your tomatoes, worms and flies will be repelled.

🌿

Each day try to work smarter
not harder.

Pets & Pests

No more itches
and scratches

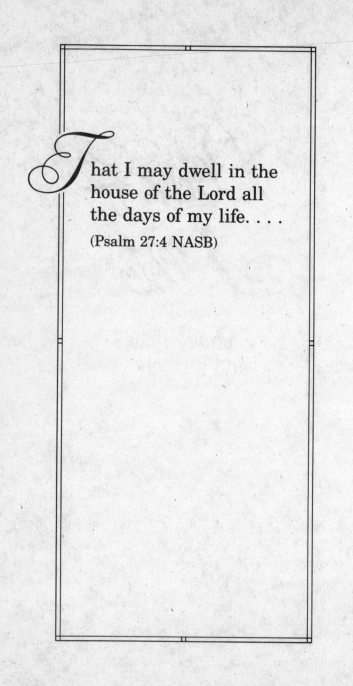

That I may dwell in the house of the Lord all the days of my life. . . .

(Psalm 27:4 NASB)

Finding accommodations when you are traveling with a pet is often time-consuming and wasteful. Avoid the hassle with "Touring With Towser," a directory of United States motels and hotels that accept guests with pets. The 64-page directory lists names, addresses, and phone numbers of 2,500 independent hotels and motels plus more than 4,000 chain locations where pets are welcome. "Touring With Towser" costs $1.50 from Gaines TWT, Dept. PNP, Box 8172, Kankakee, IL 60902.

———

Hazards that can cause illness and injury to your pets may be right in your home: tinfoil, corks, cellophane wrap, sweets (chocolate can be fatal to a pet in large amounts), cleaning fluids, and rodent and bug killers. Most pets will avoid such unpleasant smelling chemicals, but your pet could walk through it and ingest the chemicals by licking its paws. Too much food is another hazard for animals. Overfeeding is particularly dangerous to fish. Uneaten food will drop to the bottom of your aquarium and contaminate the water.

———

Cockroaches and ants are among the most unwelcome and most persistent of household pests. To stop ants from invading the kitchen, wash or spray countertops, cabinets, and floors with equal parts of vinegar and water. Planting peppermint around all entrances to your house also deters ants. For cockroaches, powdered boric acid is an effective killer. Also, distributing bay leaves around the pantry and on shelves will help keep roaches away.

———

Insect stings can be fatal if you are allergic to them. Keep an anaphylaxis emergency kit on hand if you know you are sensitive. To help avoid insect stings and bites, don't walk barefoot outdoors, stay away from flower beds, close car windows, avoid brightly colored clothing and perfumes.

A quick way to remove a swarm of flies from your house is by using your hand-held vacuum near them. The suction of the hose will pull them right into the bag.

For bee stings, make a paste using meat tenderizer and apply immediately. It will remove the stinger.

To keep ants out of cupboards, place cucumber peel on shelves.

Save your eggshells to get rid of snail and slug pests. After cracking the eggshells, wash them clean and set them out in the sun to dry. When they are dry, crumble the eggshells into small pieces and scatter over your infested areas.

Before traveling with a cat or dog: Fill a plastic bag (the self-sealing type) with ice cubes, close it tight, and put it into a bowl. Poke a couple of holes in the bag so that as the ice melts, water seeps into the bowl for drinking.

To pick up any disposable untouchable without having to

touch or wash anything, place several plastic bread bags over your hand and lower arm (like a fingerless glove). Then pick up the untouchable with the gloved hand, hold firmly, and pull the bag down off your arm and over the object to be discarded.

Try using whole cloves (the spice) in your wardrobe or when storing clothing. Silverfish, moths, and other little critters will say "bye, bye!"

Rub bug bites with a wet bar of soap to help relieve itching.

When feeding your pet, open both ends of the canned food and push one end of the food through the can into the feeding dish. If your pet eats only half of a can, simply take a knife and cut off what he can eat and replace the ends of the can, or cover ends with plastic lids or aluminum foil.

We have a cocker spaniel and his fur can be difficult to brush after his bath. So I use an inexpensive cream rinse. It works great.

If your dog has burrs, remove by working oil into the tangled area or crush burrs with pliers. Once crushed, the burrs can be combed out.

When your dog needs a pill, push the tablet into a piece

of hamburger meat, chunk of dog food, or piece of chocolate candy.

You can apply a poultice of baking soda and water to a bee sting, or apply a freshly cut slice of onion to the sting to help draw out the poison. Hold the onion in place with tape.

If you have problems with ants around your house, simply pour boiling water on each anthill. No more ants.

If you are hounded by stray dogs attacking the garbage, sprinkle full-strength ammonia over the garbage bags before placing them in the pail.

It seems that flies love garbage cans. So hose the cans down well and let them dry in the sun. Then sprinkle some dry soap powder on the bottoms of the cans.

Use hair spray to get rid of pesty flies, bees, and insects in the house. It stiffens their wings so they can't fly and down they go.

After bathing your dog, add a little vinegar or lemon juice to the rinse water. This cuts soap film and shampoo odors.

For whiter fur, put a teaspoon of bluing in the dog's shampoo or rinse water.

———

Pet spots—Try to blot up as much of the moisture with a towel as possible. Wipe with vinegar and sudsy water. Blot again. Saturate with club soda. Wipe again and again until all moisture is gone. Ammonia can be used as the last method; usually the pet won't return to the same spot.

———

Deodorize cat litter by covering the bottom of the litter pan with one part baking soda and three parts litter to absorb odors for up to a week.

———

To keep those mosquitoes away when sleeping outdoors, take a lump of sugar and wet it with several drops of spirits of camphor purchased at your pharmacy. Those critters will leave you alone.

———

During cold winter months when bathing our dog is difficult, we simply rub baking soda thoroughly into his coat and then brush it. The baking soda not only cleans, it helps get rid of doggy odor.

———

Reflector tape on your dog's or cat's collar will help your pet to be seen by drivers after dark.

———

Do you have a chewing pet? Simply purchase some oil of

cloves at your drugstore and apply to his favorite chewing spots. Animals hate the taste and the odor.

———

If a skunk sprays your pet, wash the pet in tomato juice, then shampoo. Add equal parts water and vinegar. Rinse well with this solution and then with clear water.

———

Cats hate plastic coverings, so cover the furniture you don't want them to get on with plastic. Soon they won't come near it.

———

Cats will keep away from mothballs. So stuff a few in cushions of a chair or sofa you don't want them to come near.

———

To remove ticks, soak the tick with alcohol, petroleum jelly, or oil. Wait 20 minutes for the tick to ease its grip. Grasp the tick with tweezers, near the head, gently pull it out of the skin, and place it in a jar of alcohol. Never smash a tick, as the eggs will hatch.

———

This is for the folks out there who feed our feathered friends. Pour the bag of birdseed into your large watering can. This makes it easy and neat to pour into any size bird feeder. First make sure the seed will fit through the spout of the can.

———

Most flea collars have to be trimmed to fit your pet. Save

the excess and put it in your vacuum cleaner bag to kill any fleas that find their way into the vacuum as you clean.

❧

Animals are such agreeable friends;
they ask no questions,
they make no criticisms.

Auto

Car crazy

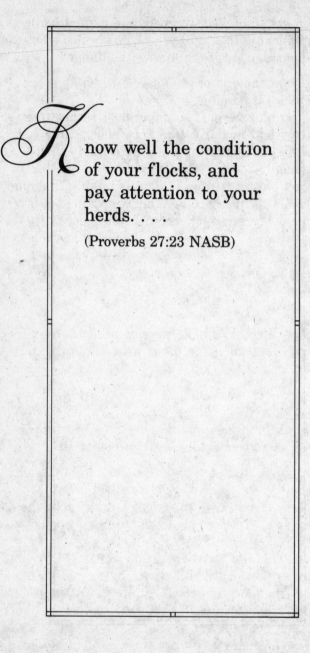

*K*now well the condition of your flocks, and pay attention to your herds. . . .

(Proverbs 27:23 NASB)

Cars often get scratched, scraped, and dented while parked in parking lots. State Farm Insurance offers these defensive parking tips to minimize the danger:

- —Park at the end of the lot or away from other vehicles if possible.
- —Select a space next to a four-door rather than a two-door model. Doors of two-door cars swing out farther and are more likely to do damage.
- —Don't park next to a junker. It's likely that the driver will not care whether his vehicle gets another scratch—or whether yours does.
- —Pull you car into the space as far as possible so you won't be hit by someone backing out from the other side.

I could never find my car in big parking lots. Now I tie a strip of red material to the top of my radio antenna, and by looking for my red flag, I can easily spot my vehicle.

To prevent children from getting restless on long car rides, keep them comfortable and entertained.

- —Frequent stops are important; try to make them before the kids get fidgety.
- —Treat older kids to snacks, but make sure they run around for ten to 15 minutes before setting off again.
- —Let kids take turns riding up front.
- —Keep a "surprise bag" ready. Bring out toys and treats one at a time. Small novelties are good. Choose snacks that aren't too messy like apples, cookies, and cheese.
- —Play the radio and tapes. Join in a sing-along.

—Point out new sights—farm animals, forests, rivers, passing trains.

—Play a few observation games. Preschoolers can spot cars of different colors. Older children can find out-of-state vehicles or try to identify automobile models on the road.

Every time I need to get directions to a place, I write them out on a 3 x 5 card. I keep an envelope of these directions in the glove compartment of my car. I also write the return directions on the other side so I don't have to reverse them in my mind on the way back.

I tape a transparent plastic 3 x 5 sleeve to the middle of my steering wheel. When I have to go someplace unfamiliar, I find the right card and slip it in the sleeve. I never have to figure out the directions twice, and with the sleeve, the directions are in sight for quick reference during the trip.

When you wash your car, use two large, old bath towels to wipe and dry the windows and car exterior. They get quite dirty so instead of putting them in the washing machine, put them in a pail of water with detergent. A little up-and-down motion with a drain plunger works like magic. Do the same in the rinse water. (A bucket, plunger, and cold-water detergent should be great for campers to take along, too.)

Grungy-looking car upholstery? Scrub with a solution of one tablespoon washing soda per quart of warm water. Rinse using clear water and a sponge. Blot up excess with an old towel and then leave car doors open for a few minutes to hasten drying. Cheap and effective!

Be sure to carry a small dry chemical fire extinguisher in your car. This might save your car from being destroyed by an unexpected fire.

———

I keep a small spray bottle filled with window cleaner and a roll of paper towels in my car. I have found this especially helpful on a long trip when bugs have accumulated on the windshield between stops at service stations.

———

A good idea to prove the ownership of your car is to print your name, address, and phone number on a 3 x 5 card (or use your business card) and slide it down your car window on the driver's side. If your car is lost or stolen, you can prove it is yours.

———

Baking soda quickly cleans spatters and traffic grime from windshields, headlights, chrome, and enamel. Wipe with soda sprinkled onto a damp sponge. Rinse.

———

Most auto accidents occur at speeds less than 40 mph, within 25 miles of home, and on dry roads.

The impact of a car accident is over in one-tenth of a second—you have no time to brace yourself, much less to protect your child.

———

The trunk is an excellent place to carry material for emergency situations. You might include fuses, jumper cables, flares, screwdriver, extra fan belt and spark plugs, flashlight, first-aid kit, fire extinguisher, blanket, towel, rope, and bottled water.

Your floor mats can be used to keep windshields from freezing. Put them on the outside on front windows. Use your wipers to hold them in place.

In snow areas, keep a bag of kitty litter in your trunk. The litter can be scattered to give traction if your car gets stuck in the snow.

When driving in your automobile, listen to inspirational radio or cassette tape programs. Listen to self-development programs of an educational nature. Automobiles are the best rolling universities in the world.

To save dollars at the gas pumps during the cold winter months: Give your car a chance to warm up at idle. A cold engine under normal road conditions will burn 10 to 20 percent more gas than it should. Check the thermostat if your car is slow to warm up. This temperature-activated device controls the water from the radiator to the engine, providing a cooler flow in summer and a warmer flow in winter. Flush the cooling system if you still have warm-up problems. It may be clogged. Most owner's manuals recommend draining and flushing the cooling system about once every two years. Ensure your tires are properly inflated. If not, you may be wasting hundreds of miles' worth of gasoline—probably enough for a short vacation. Riding on underinflated tires robs you of half a mile for every gallon of gas, and ruins your tires. To find the proper level of inflation for your tires, check your owner's manual. A manufacturer's plate containing the same information is usually located on the driver's side doorjamb. Change spark plugs every 25,000 miles. If one plug out of eight is misfiring, you are losing an eighth of the engine's output each time you step on the gas.

Instead of washing your car with soap and water, try washing with a bucket of water and one cup kerosene, followed by a good wiping with soft cloths. The best part of it is that no matter how dirty your car is, it will not need wetting down before you start, nor rinsing once you have finished. When it rains, the car will actually bead off water. It helps prevent rust. Use no wax with this method. Great for chrome.

Hide a key for the times you lock your keys inside the car. Caution: Don't put it under the hood if you have an inside hood release.

To remove bumper stickers, use nail polish remover or lighter fluid. Gently scrape away with a razor blade or knife.

Use plastic net bags (the kind onions come in) to wash windshields when insects have accumulated. Simply tie a few bags into one big bag and rub away.

If you have bumped the front fender of your car into the back wall of your garage, try this: Suspend a small rubber ball on a string from the ceiling of the garage so that when the ball strikes your windshield, you will know the car is far enough in to close the garage door.

Keep a first-aid kit in your trunk. Make the kit by filling an empty coffee can with bandages, aspirin, antiseptic, scissors, safety pins, tweezers, thermometer, adhesive tape, gauze, cotton balls, and Q-tips. Cover it with the plastic lid. It takes up little room and yet holds a lot of supplies.

We don't have a garage and have several cars. This past winter someone said rubbing alcohol would defrost the ice on the windows. After the first time I tried it, I decided to put the alcohol in a small spray bottle. It works as well as any of the over-the-counter defrosting sprays.

To remove price sheets from your car window, liberally sponge hot vinegar onto the sheets. Scrape gently. Continue applying vinegar until sheet is gone. Lemon extract works well too, or apply salad oil, allowing it to set for a while before scraping the sheet away.

To prevent corrosion on your auto battery, scrub the terminals and holder with a strong solution of baking soda and water. Then smear with petroleum jelly.

Before you call someone to start your car on cold

mornings, blow hot air on the carburetor from a hair dryer. It works.

―――――

A plastic credit card makes a wonderful frost, ice, and snow scraper for your windows and rearview mirrors.

―――――

I've always had trouble remembering to turn my car headlights off after driving in rainy or foggy weather. I solved this problem by purchasing a brightly colored clip, the type used for clipboards, to place on my ignition each time I turn my lights on in unusual weather conditions. After I've parked and reached to turn off the engine, I have an instant reminder that never fails me. When the clip is not in use I fasten it around my turn-signal bar. Easily reached when needed but out of the way when not.

―――――

I know the trend is toward car pooling, but I try to avoid it because it wastes a lot of my time. People are never ready at the same time. Someone is always waiting. If you must car pool, learn to do things while you wait: balance the checkbook, write letters, read a book or paper, memorize Scripture, and so forth.

―――――

When taking a trip with children, a shoe bag or a homemade bag can be hung on the back of the front seat or on the car door to store crayons, scissors, glue, jump rope (for rest and gas stops), games, and miscellaneous items.

―――――

Cigarette ashes that continue to burn in the car ashtray

are a nuisance. Prevent this by placing an inch of baking soda in the bottom of the tray.

For emergencies, make a sign to keep in your car that says, "CALL THE POLICE." You never know when it may be needed.

To open a frozen lock, heat the key with a cigarette lighter or match. Never force the key. Turn very gently.

Soak tar spots with raw linseed oil. Allow to stand until soft. Then wipe with a soft cloth that has been dampened with the oil.

To cover up scratches, take a matching color crayon and work into the scratch well.

With three children, car trips used to be an ordeal for my parents. So my dad started presenting each of us with "fun money"—a roll of dimes apiece—when we pulled out of the driveway. For each "How much farther?" or "He's poking me!" or "She's got her leg on my side of the car!" we spoke, Dad would charge a dime. Whatever we had left when we reached our destination was ours to spend. This cut squabbles to a minimum.

The noises your car makes are its way of telling you it

has a problem. Listen carefully, and you will save time, repair bills, and perhaps even your life. Listen for: *a high-pitched tinkling sound when you accelerate*. You could be running your engine on the wrong grade of gas. Check the owner's manual for the recommended grade. If the noise continues, have it checked at a garage. *A banging noise in the exhaust system*. That is a backfire and could mean it's time for new spark plugs or that the fuel mixture is too lean. *A coughing sound as the engine is turned off*. Your carburetor probably needs adjusting. *Squeaking noises from the brakes*. This is often the result of damp weather. If the noise continues or you hear grating and groaning, have all brakes checked.

If your oil warning light stays on, it could mean that your oil pressure is low. Running a car without oil will cause the engine to seize and ruin the engine. Stop immediately.

I live in a damp area with no garage. Dew often covers the car windows. I dislike the time it takes to go back inside for paper towels, so I keep an oven mitt in the back of the car and slip it on to wipe the windows. It dries fast and I don't waste my time.

Since I am on emergency call quite often, I can't take the necessary time to pack an overnight tote bag, so I have one packed and in my automobile trunk for those urgent calls. Saves a lot of time.

When black rubber tape or plastic trim on your car fades

or gets white spots, use black shoe polish to freshen the trim. It will look new again.

––––––––––

Keep a new, clean chalkboard eraser handy to wipe the inside windows when moisture collects on them.

––––––––––

Have an extra set of keys. Keep extra house and car keys in your wallet or other accessible place. If you lock yourself out, you'll save time and trouble by using your spare keys.

––––––––––

Always keep five to ten pennies and a few nickels, dimes, and quarters in the glove compartment. It's very handy when you don't have the correct pocket change for the parking meter or the toll roads.

––––––––––

Make sure your glove compartment has a good supply of materials as you head off on your vacation trips. You might have: maps; notepad and pen; tire pressure gauge; premoistened wipes; sunglasses; reading material; can opener; plastic forks, knives, and spoons; change for telephone calls; business cards; matches; scissors; nail clippers; and first-aid kit.

––––––––––

Ice or snow will not stick to your windshield if you rub some moistened salt over the outside.

––––––––––

Emergency precaution: Apply large strips of fluorescent

tape diagonally across the inside top of your car trunk. If you need to stop on the highway at night, open your trunk, and you have a warning sign.

———

While traveling, I find it handy to keep a large resealable freezer bag in the car for trash. It keeps the car clean of sticky wrappers and empty containers, and anything left in the containers will not spill during a quick stop.

———

A great idea for removing car grease from your hands: Use some vegetable shortening (used for cooking). A little soap and water remove the shortening.

———

When traveling with children, I spread a large sheet over the backseat and floor. When I get gas or come to a rest stop, I just take out the sheet and shake it. That way crumbs, wrappers, and dirt come out of the car. (Remember to pick up the papers and drop them into a trash can.)

❧

*The worst fault of a motorist
is his belief that he has none.*

Miscellaneous

More
bright ideas

*L*et heaven fill your thoughts; don't spend your time worrying about things down here.

(Colossians 3:2)

When I travel, it never fails that I forget some small but vital toiletry item. So now, when I have overnight guests, I fill a wicker basket with sample-size bottles of shampoo and conditioner, toothpaste, a disposable razor, and other items. Then I place the basket in the spare bathroom with a note for my guests to help themselves.

File pencil erasers that have been worn smooth with an emery board to roughen the surface and make them work like new.

If your draperies gap in the middle when you close them, sew a small magnet into each of the center seams. Then simply press the magnets together for a tight closing.

For sticky locks, or when your key doesn't go into the lock easily, use a lead pencil to coat the edges of the key with graphite. It really works. Never use oil.

A wonderful wedding gift to give to an in-law is a calendar with the names and birthdays of the immediate members of the "new family." This calendar reminds them when to send cards or gifts so they arrive on time.

To avoid opening used cans of paint to see if enough is left for another job, make a mark on the outside of the can at the paint level, using the color of the paint in the can.

Here's an easy way to erase paint splatters from a brick fireplace: Get a broken brick the same color as the brick on the fireplace and scrub it back and forth over the spattered areas. Brick against brick will abrade most of the paint.

When I receive a wedding invitation I place the date on my present calendar and also place it on next year's calendar. That way I at least send a card on the first anniversary. The couple will be delighted.

Keep a clothespin in the bathroom to hang your shower cap to dry.

Keep your razor blades in a jar of alcohol; they don't rust and the blades will last for ages.

Extra wallpaper is great to use for gift wrapping or covering boxes for storage in a closet. They look pretty and blend well.

Wallpaper scraps are useful. It's always a good idea to save some scraps in case a section of the paper needs to be repaired later. To make a patch, tear (don't cut) a scrap into the approximate size and shape needed. The irregular torn edges will blend better with the paper already on the wall than would the edges of a cut patch.

A small cup hook makes a good seal for an open tube of

glue, cement, or wood putty. It also furnishes a
convenient way to hang the tube on a wall or shelf.

I always carry a small pocket magnifying glass in my
purse. If I forget to bring my reading glasses when
shopping, I have a good substitute to read labels with.

Keep a "company" notebook. Make a page for each family
that you invite to your home for a meal or snack. List
date, menu, and specific notes regarding preferences or
needs in food. Example: Jim doesn't like tomatoes.
Claudia: hypoglycemic—no sugar. This helps to plan for
the next time and avoids repeating the same meal.

Address all birthday and anniversary cards for each
month at one time; then in the corner where the stamp
goes, put the date it needs to be mailed. Keep them in an
obvious place so you don't forget.

Make your phone book attractive by covering it with
leftover wallpaper or fabrics that coordinate with colors of
the room.

An idea for grandparents: Take a cardboard box and cover
it with fabric or wallpaper to coordinate with your room.
Fill it with fun toys, games, and books, making it a
"Grandma's and Grandpa's Box." When children come to
visit, you always have some safe things they can play
with, rather than your china cups and saucers.

To prevent your rocker or kitchen chairs from scratching your waxed, wooden floors, line the bottoms with adhesive tape or wax the bottoms.

With leftover fabric, make gift bags in all sizes. Use pinking shears for the top and tie a string or ribbon around the top to secure it. Great for Christmas jams, jellies, breads, or any bottled items.

Use fresh flowers; sprigs of mint, holly, Creeping Charlie; or a small pine branch to give your gift a special touch.

When purchasing gift wrap, get an all-occasion print. For instance, red and white polka dot can be used at Christmas with a green bow, Valentine's Day with a red bow, springtime with a yellow bow, and summer and Fourth of July with a blue bow. One wrap for all occasions.

Use a brown lunch sack to gift wrap odd-shaped items. Fluff a crisp sheet of colored tissue paper out of the top and tie with a ribbon. Simply adorable!

One grandmother wrote that she saves the newspaper the day each grandchild is born. She will present it to the child or mother for a keepsake.

Leftover washable wallpaper can be cut in desired sizes and used as washable placemats.

You can "shrink" a sagging cane chair seat back into shape. Wait for a sunny day. Then wet the caned area only with a cloth dipped in hot water. The cane should be as wet as you can get it, but don't let the water come into contact with the wood sections of the chair. Place the chair out-of-doors in the strong sun to dry.

❧

Don't pile it—file it.

You may obtain seminar information or a price list of materials available by sending your request and a self-addressed, stamped envelope to:

MORE HOURS IN MY DAY
2838 Rumsey Drive
Riverside, CA 92506

Share your favorite hints with us!
Submission of hints by readers constitutes permission for accepted hints to be printed in future publications.

*Other Good
Harvest House Reading*

THE COMPLETE HOLIDAY ORGANIZER
A Busy Woman's Guide to Holiday Planning
by *Emilie Barnes*

The Complete Holiday Organizer is an invaluable aid to creating treasured holiday memories. It's the busy woman's answer to holiday planning. Birthdays, Valentine's Day, Mother's Day, Thanksgiving, and Christmas are just a few of the holidays Emilie covers, giving ideas and helpful hints to make preparation easier. A brief history about each holiday will challenge you to begin your own family traditions and memories. A practical "how-to" book to help you get a handle on holiday organization.

1988 DAILY PLANNER
With Friendship Thoughts To Brighten Each Day
by *Emilie Barnes*

Get organized and stay organized with this handy purse-sized daily calendar. The easy-to-use format has space for important dates, goals, accomplishments, and prayer requests, and includes helpful hints on becoming a better friend. The convenient spiral binding keeps pages lying flat for ease in note-taking.

EATING RIGHT!
A Realistic Approach to a Healthy Lifestyle
by *Emilie Barnes and Sue Gregg*
Confused by one fad diet after another and the conflicting advice from nutritionists about what to eat? Bestselling author Emilie Barnes and home economist Sue Gregg approach the conflicts involved in food selection, preparation, and kitchen organization with practical help and a *realistic* approach based on common-sense guidelines and God's plan for healthy eating. Develop an "eating lifestyle" that really works!

EMILIE'S HOUSEHOLD HINTS
by *Emilie Barnes*

What women need to know to save time and energy around the home and enjoy more organized and productive days.

MORE HOURS IN MY DAY
by *Emilie Barnes*

There can be more hours in your day when you use the collection of calendars, charts, and guides in this useful book on home time management.

SURVIVAL FOR BUSY WOMEN
Establishing Efficient Home Management
by *Emilie Barnes*

A hands-on manual for establishing a more efficient home-management program. Over 25 charts and forms can be personalized to help you organize your home.

Dear Reader:

We would appreciate hearing from you regarding this Harvest House nonfiction book. It will enable us to continue to give you the best in Christian publishing.

1. What most influenced you to purchase *The Creative Home Organizer?*
   - ☐ Author
   - ☐ Subject matter
   - ☐ Backcover copy
   - ☐ Recommendations
   - ☐ Cover/Title
   - ☐ _____

2. Where did you purchase this book?
   - ☐ Christian bookstore
   - ☐ General bookstore
   - ☐ Other
   - ☐ Grocery store
   - ☐ Department store

3. Your overall rating of this book:
   ☐ Excellent ☐ Very good ☐ Good ☐ Fair ☐ Poor

4. How likely would you be to purchase other books by this author?
   - ☐ Very likely
   - ☐ Somewhat likely
   - ☐ Not very likely
   - ☐ Not at all

5. What types of books most interest you?
   (check all that apply)
   - ☐ Women's Books
   - ☐ Marriage Books
   - ☐ Current Issues
   - ☐ Self Help/Psychology
   - ☐ Bible Studies
   - ☐ Fiction
   - ☐ Biographies
   - ☐ Children's Books
   - ☐ Youth Books
   - ☐ Other _____

6. Please check the box next to your age group.
   - ☐ Under 18
   - ☐ 18-24
   - ☐ 25-34
   - ☐ 35-44
   - ☐ 45-54
   - ☐ Over 55

Mail to: Editorial Director
Harvest House Publishers
1075 Arrowsmith
Eugene, OR 97402

Name _____

Address _____

City _____ State _____ Zip _____

Thank you for helping us to help you in future publications!